SPOOKY
California

Tales of Hauntings, Strange Happenings, and Other Local Lore

RETOLD BY S. E. SCHLOSSER

ILLUSTRATED BY PAUL G. HOFFMAN

INSIDERS' GUIDE®

GUILFORD, CONNECTICUT

AN IMPRINT OF THE GLOBE PEQUOT PRESS

For my family: David, Dena, Tim, Arlene, Hannah, Emma, Nathan, Benjamin, Deb, Gabe, Clare, Jack, and Karen.

For the lunch crowd: Sasa, Drazen, Dieter, Dirk, Hui, Judy, and Dennis. Thanks for keeping me laughing!

***

INSIDERS' GUIDE®

Text design by Lisa Reneson
Illustrations and map border by Paul G. Hoffman
Map © The Globe Pequot Press

Library of Congress Cataloging-in-Publication Data:
Schlosser, S.E.
  Spooky California: tales of hauntings, strange happenings, and other local lore/retold by S.E. Schlosser; illustrations by Paul G. Hoffman. —1st ed.
      p. cm.
  Includes bibliographical references.
  ISBN 0-7627-3844-8
  1. Folklore—California. 2. Tales—California. 3. Haunted places— California. I Title.
  GR110.C3S34 2005
  398'/09794—dc22

                                                                2005015515

Manufactured in the United States of America
First Edition/Second Printing

Contents

SPOOKY SITES . . .

AND WHERE TO FIND THEM

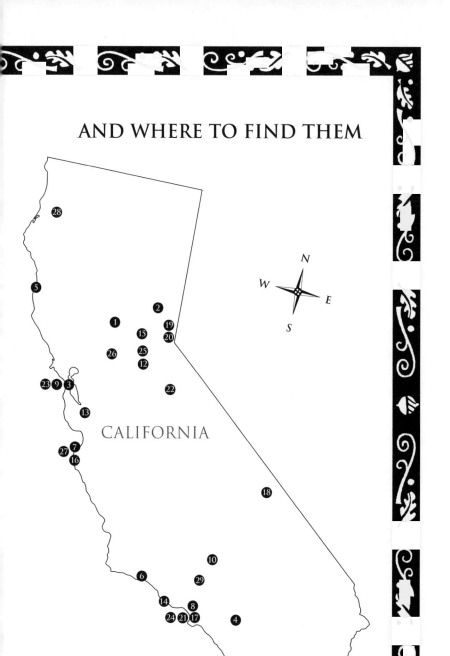

CALIFORNIA

Contents

Introduction

What's so spooky about California? Isn't this the land of sunshine, Hollywood, and beautiful vistas? Indeed it is! But it is also the place where Bigfoot roams in the north woods; where the spirits of Argonauts still pan for gold; where a dead mother still attends to the needs of her new-born infant; and where a ghost ship sails across the desert on the invisible waters of a long-dead sea.

As I child, I visited California with my grandparents on a cross-country RV trip. My first memories of this beautiful state consist of very tall trees, a pumpkin coach, and a large conch shell—the biggest shell I had ever found. (Hey, I was only six!)

My first trip to California as an adult was to Monterey. I am the quintessential tourist—I could be in the darkest reaches of the Amazon, and instinct would lead me unerringly to the one village where some enterprising local had set up a tour of the huts, a hot dog stand, and a souvenir shop. So the first thing I did when I arrived was to sign up for a bus tour of Monterey and Carmel. The history of the missions, the story of the former capital of California, and the way the land changed as it moved from Spanish hands to Mexican and finally to American fascinated me. But what I enjoyed most about Monterey and the surrounding towns was the plethora of spooky stories that haunted the area.

Perhaps my favorite Monterey–Carmel folktale is the story in which a priest is attacked by a thief on his way to minister to a sick member of his parish. The thief is brought to a very harsh sort of justice, thanks to a hen and her chicks. Then there is the tale of the Lady in Lace, who haunts the roadways near Pebble Beach. Though my guided tour took me along the Seventeen Mile Drive and passed the Ghost Tree, I alas, did not spot this mysterious spirit.

Carmel and Monterey are not the only spooky spots in California. A blood-stain appears on the porch of a haunted house near Fort Bragg just before the manifestation of the murder victim; the ghostly Jake and his camels roam the Sierra Nevada; a headless man longs for his lover in Hollywood; a serpent lurks beneath the waters of Lake Tahoe; and the devil pays a visit to a prisoner in Los Angeles.

I remember spending one memorable evening, during a recent trip to San Francisco, chasing the supernatural on a local ghost tour. Though our trail led us up and down the streets of San Francisco, I did not manage to bump into the ghost of the bandit Joaquin, the spirit of murdered Ishi (Vengeance), or the bogeyman who cannot seem to keep track of his head.

A large number of spooky stories in California focus on treasure of one sort or another. In one story a miner strikes it rich, thanks to the assistance of the Tommy Knockers. Of course, some weren't so lucky. In another story one of the Argonauts takes over the claim of a dead miner and finds himself being chased out by a very angry ghost! Then there is the story from San Diego, in which the sound of phantom bells may guide listeners to buried treasure—or to their deaths, depending on which version you choose to believe.

As an adult, it took me maybe thirty seconds to fall in love with California. I don't know if it was the architecture, the history, or the warm sunshine and cool breezes, but I was caught—hook, line, and sinker—from the moment I arrived in Monterey, and my infatuation only grew with subsequent visits to both Northern and Southern California. I really cannot blame the old-timer who retired in Sacramento and found the balmy climate of California so much to his liking that he just never did get around to dying. His great-great grandchildren finally encouraged him to travel outside the state, and sure enough, he died after living for a few weeks on the East Coast. 'Course, his relatives then made the mistake of bringing him back to California to be buried. . . . Now when I retire, I'm going to move into the house right next door to that old-timer, and believe me, I won't make the mistake of letting my great-great-grandkids send me on a trip out-of-state. No sir!

—Sandy Schlosser

PART ONE
Ghost Stories

1

Milk Bottles

I took over the family business when my father died—we owned the most successful grocery in town—and money was coming in hand-over-fist, until the Great Depression hit. Even then, things weren't too bad for me and the missus. After all, people still needed food and supplies to go on living, so the townsfolk kept coming to our store. I kept prices reasonable, unlike some of my fellow merchants, so folks came to us long after the other stores went out of business. We managed to scrape by with enough food to feed our twin sons, and even had a small toy or two to give them at Christmas. My wife had a talent for making wonderful toys out of the odds and ends leftover at the store, which came in real handy during the holidays.

Yes, we had a good life, even in those hard times. Our only sorrow was the lack of a little daughter in our lives. The doctor told me and the missus that we couldn't have any more children. "One less mouth to feed," my wife said bravely when she heard the news, but I knew she was smarting inside. Every once in a while, when one of our customers came into the store with their baby girl, my wife would get teary-eyed and duck into the back room to compose herself. Sometimes she wouldn't come out until the baby was gone. I wanted to help her, but what could I say? I was smarting inside, too.

About a month after our visit to the doctor, a new face appeared in my store. A small, thin woman with dark hair, a narrow face, and faded blue eyes stood peering in the window. Just another poor, bedraggled woman, struggling to feed her family, I thought. I saw them all the time, their faces careworn and blank. The Great Depression had created hundreds of them. Seeing them always reminded me that I was one of the lucky ones who still had enough money to feed my family.

I knew all my customers, as well as everyone who lived and worked in the neighborhood, but I had never seen this woman before. She must be one of the migrant workers, come to town to help with the harvest, I thought. Here for a few weeks and then gone with the wind.

After hesitating on the doorstep for a few moments, she came into my shop carrying two empty milk bottles. Wordlessly, she placed them on the counter in front of me. I gazed into her eyes, waiting for her to ask for something. She just stood there, looking at me hopefully. Perhaps she doesn't speak English, I thought. I took the empty bottles and replaced them with full bottles. Taking in her tattered dress and worn face, I asked for only half the going price. I wasn't really surprised when she did not reply. Probably, she had no money at all.

I watched her pick up the milk bottles and leave the shop. I suppose I could have gone after her to demand my money, or called the police, but I did neither. I saw the need in her care-

MILK BOTTLES

worn face. A long time ago, I had decided that no one in my neighborhood was going to starve. Not while my grocery was still open.

The woman was back the next day with two empty milk bottles. She placed them on the counter, still wordless. Again I looked deep into her eyes as I replaced the empty bottles with full ones. Again, she took the milk without paying and hurried out the door. She looked so worried that I began to wonder if she had a job at all. Perhaps someone at home was sick, and she'd had to quit her job to nurse them. That night over dinner I told my wife about the woman. She suggested that I offer the woman a part-time position cleaning the store if she came again. I was pleased with her suggestion, and decided to do so at the next opportunity. My wife is a gem of a woman! Given the chance, I would marry her again.

The woman came the next morning. For the third time, she exchanged her empty bottles for full without saying a word. I tried to talk to her, telling her about the part-time position cleaning the store, but she acted as if she did not hear me. Her blue eyes were desperate, and she practically ran from the store with the milk. Her urgency worried me. I hesitated for a moment, then closed up the grocery and followed her, wondering what I could do to help.

To my surprise, the woman headed away from the migrant camp. She walked rapidly, head down, across town and went into the local graveyard. I followed, puzzled. What was she doing here? As I watched, the woman hurried up to a stone marker and then disappeared into the ground! I rubbed my eyes in disbelief. She had melted into the ground, like a . . . like a ghost. I shivered, suddenly chilled by what I had seen. And then I heard the muffled cry of a baby coming from the ground underneath the stone marker where the woman had disappeared! It was a weary cry, as if the baby had been weeping for a long time and no longer expected anyone to come to it.

For a long moment, I was frozen to the spot. Then I came to my senses and ran back to the store to phone the police. Within minutes, the graveyard was swarming with people. Several workers started digging up the grave where I had heard the crying. When the casket was opened, I saw the woman who had visited my store lying dead within it. In her arms, she held a small baby girl and two full milk bottles. The infant was still alive.

The police rushed the baby to the hospital, where she spent several days being nursed back to health. I brought my wife several times to visit the tyke while she was at the hospital. We spoke to the proper authorities about adopting her, as she had no family other than the mother with whom she had been buried. By the time she was ready to leave the hospital, she was officially ours. We named her Helen, which was the name on her mother's grave. We still have the milk bottles that her mother's ghost used to save her life. When she is older, we will tell her the story.

2

The Spook of Misery Hill

No one ever thought Jim Brandon would amount to much. Kinder folks called him thriftless. His creditors used less kindly terms, and Jim would walk the other way if he saw any of them approaching. So we were all surprised when Jim took it in his head to work the abandoned mine on Misery Hill. Old Tom Bowers used to own the Misery Hill claim. He was a bit of a hermit, Tom was. He stayed out by the mine and didn't come to town much; he didn't like the rough crowd that gathered there to drink and spend their gold unwisely. One day Old Tom went missing, and we found him buried under a landslide. Despite a decent burial, Old Tom's ghost kept walking around the mouth of the mine at night, scaring anyone who went near it. At least, that's what folks claimed.

Well, Jim Brandon decided the stories about the mine were all rot. He set to his mining with an industry of spirit quite out of character for him. He got the mine up and running lickety-split, started paying off his creditors, and began making a name for himself among his fellow miners.

One day Jim came into the bar and complained bitterly about some upstart who was working the claim behind his back.

"How can you tell?" asked Red Thompson, one of Jim's buddies.

"Every morning when I get to the mine, the sluice is open and the water's turned on," Jim growled. "I've searched high and low for that no-good claim jumper. Just wait until I get my hands on him!"

"Sounds like somebody's playing a joke on you," Red said calmly.

"They'll wish they hadn't messed about with me when I get through with them," said Jim, slamming his fist down on top of the bar for emphasis.

"Maybe it's Old Tom Bowers, come back to work his claim," Lester Mann called out from his place farther down the bar.

"That's nonsense," Jim Brandon replied, and stomped out of the bar.

Everyone chuckled a bit at the joke being played on Jim, and then forgot about it. But Jim was sure it wasn't a joke. Someone was jumping his claim, and he aimed to stop it. That night, Jim loaded up his rifle and crept noiselessly toward his camp, waiting for the claim jumper to appear. The wind was whispering eerily through the trees overhead, and the moonlight kept flitting in and out of the clouds. Jim's skin prickled and he gave a sudden shiver of fear. There was no sound except for the wind and the murmur of the river. No night creature called; no hoot from an owl. Jim didn't like it one bit.

The moon disappeared behind a large cloud. In the darkness, Jim saw something shining ahead of him. Goose bumps broke out on his skin. Jim had to draw a few calming breaths and mutter aloud "I don't believe in ghosts" several times before he felt calm enough to walk toward the light. As he drew near, he saw a glowing piece of paper tacked to the trunk of a tamarack tree. The words on the paper said: NOTICE! I, THOMAS BOWERS, CLAIM THIS LAND FOR PLACER MINING.

Jim reeled backward with a gasp of terror, and crouched down on the ground with his head between his knees for several long moments. "I don't believe in ghosts," he mumbled over and over again. Suddenly, he was angry. That claim jumper is trying to play tricks on my mind, he thought. He leapt to his feet and reached out to rip the paper from the tree trunk. Immediately, the strength left his arm and it fell limp at his side.

Jim stood frozen in place, his body shaking. He closed his eyes, trying to convince himself that there was no notice on the tree. It was just a trick of the moonlight. When he opened his eyes, the glowing notice was gone!

Jim drew in a shuddering breath, trying to pretend that everything was normal. Then he heard it: the sound of water flowing through a sluice and the crunch of a pick in gravel! The glowing notice was instantly forgotten. Jim clutched his rifle and hurried toward the sluice. Behind him, the glowing notice reappeared on the tree, lighting the path toward the Misery Hill mine.

Jim rounded the final corner and saw a man working at the sluice. He brought his gun to his shoulder and took aim. As he fired off a shot, he got a good look at the man. The light from the glowing notice revealed a tall, lanky man with tangled white hair and a white beard covered with dirt and debris. The man's skin was gray and rotting, and his eyes blazed within

THE SPOOK OF MISERY HILL

fathomless dark sockets. The dead face turning to look at Jim was that of Old Tom Bowers.

Jim shouted in terror as the shot passed harmlessly through the dead miner's corpse. A look of deadly fury creased the withered, rotting face. Slowly, the ghost raised his pick and shovel, pointing them at Jim. Then Old Tom sprang forward, his blazing eyes fixed on his quarry, and raced toward the terrified man. Jim screamed and ran for his life, down the hill, through the woods, ducking under tree limbs, jumping over rocks, and scrambling through scrub. He could hear Old Tom behind him, his dead feet pounding heavily on the ground. Neither the branches that pummeled Jim's face nor the rocks and rubble that tripped him seemed to bother the corpse. It was gaining on him.

Jim saw the lights of Pike City ahead. The saloon was full of miners celebrating a new find. Jim could hear them dancing and singing and laughing. He pushed himself to the limit, desperate to reach the safety of the saloon. He was almost there when a pair of withered hands closed around his shoulders, tumbling him to the ground just a few feet shy of the lighted doorway.

Inside the saloon, a horrible shriek cut through the din. The miners gasped, falling silent as the shriek rose higher and higher, hitting a note that shattered all the glasses in the saloon. Then it stopped. The men stared at each other, faces pale, bodies shaking. Some of the men's hands were bleeding from cuts they had received when their glasses shattered. A few of the bravest ventured out into the darkness. Jim Brandon's rifle lay in the road, just outside the light from the doorway. The ground around it was torn up, as if two people had been rolling and wrestling in the dirt. A few yards away, lying haphazardly, as if they had been thrown aside at the last minute, were a pick and a shovel with the letters "TB" cut into the handle. There was nothing else.

Jim Brandon was never seen again in Pike City. As for the Misery Hill mine, none of the local residents go near it, though strangers passing through often report that they have heard the sluice running there at night.

3

Vengeance

SAN FRANCISCO

When the samurai warrior Kane first came to California from Tokyo, he brought with him a new wife, the beautiful Ishi. She was an ideal wife: gentle, attentive, and obedient as well as a wonderful cook and homemaker. She always referred to Kane as "Husband" in the old style, which pleased him greatly. Kane was the envy of his new neighbors, and he and Ishi lived for several years in happiness.

But Kane was a proud man, the eldest child of indulgent parents, and he believed that nothing was too good for such a one as he. When a wealthy family of high rank moved into the neighborhood, Kane cast his eye upon their lovely daughter and desired her. The beauty and obedience of Ishi no longer pleased him. In his mind Ishi was second best, and Kane plotted to rid himself of his unwanted wife so he could woo and win the fair Aiko.

On the way home from a great banquet one stormy night, Kane pushed his young wife over the cliff into the bay. No one heard Ishi's scream through the howl of the wind and rain. No one suspected foul play when a distraught Kane came rushing

VENGEANCE

back to the banquet hall, shouting for help because his poor wife had slipped in the mud and fallen over the edge of the cliff. The searchers found Ishi's broken body at dawn. Her long, black hair was tangled with seaweed, her beautiful face was crushed by the rocks on the beach, and her teeth were shattered.

Kane acted the part of the bereaved husband to perfection. He gave Ishi a splendid funeral. It wasn't until he was alone in his house after the neighbors had all gone away that Kane relaxed and drank to his success. In a month he would woo and wed the lovely Aiko, and her wealth would become his. Kane laid himself down upon his mat, rejoicing in the absence of Ishi and dreaming of his new love.

Outside, the wind whipped against the house, making the walls rattle and shake. A stray breeze swept through the sleeping-room with a sibilant whisper: "Vengeance. Vengeance." The breeze hissed and slapped the sleeping samurai. Kane rolled over restlessly as the door to the room slowly slid open. Moonlight streamed through the doorway, waking the warrior. Kane sat up and blinked as a hideously broken figure slowly stepped into the room. The wind whipped its long, seaweed-tangled black hair over the dirty, bloodstained kimono. Its face was crushed and broken, with one eyeball hanging by a thread from the socket. The ghost of Ishi reached out a bony hand toward her husband, smiling horribly through the shattered remains of her teeth. "Vengeance," she whispered, stretching her bloodstained hand caressingly toward Kane's face. "Vengeance."

Kane screamed in terror and tripped over the mat in his haste to flee from the dreadful figure. He leapt out of the window and ran to a neighbor's house, gibbering in fear. His neighbors, mistaking his fear for overwhelming grief, welcomed him into their home and insisted he spend the rest of the night with them.

Kane tried to behave normally the next day, but as night fell his hands began to shake with fear, and he could not bring himself to enter his house. Instead, the samurai took his mat to an abandoned house in the neighborhood, determined to sleep within its ruins so that the ghost of Ishi could not find him. He left a paper lantern burning over his mat to keep away the shadows and finally fell into a dreamless sleep.

At the stroke of midnight, the wind began whipping against the abandoned house, whistling through the cracks and causing the ivy growing through a break in the wall to sway and grasp like bony, bloodstained hands. "Vengeance," the wind hissed. Kane woke with a start. Above him, the breeze tossed the lantern. The candle guttered, and the paper caught fire in several places. Slowly, two eyes burned themselves into the paper, and a wide grinning mouth with the shattered remains of teeth took shape. "Vengeance," the mouth whispered as the ivory hands reached out caressingly toward Kane. "Vengeance."

Kane grabbed his sword and hacked at the cloying, entangling vines. They were trying to strangle him, but he managed to free an arm and cut them away from his body. Above him, the face in the lantern laughed. "Vengeance," it cried. "I seek vengeance, Husband."

Kane broke free from the vines and fled from the abandoned house, followed by the sound of Ishi's laughter. He ran back to his neighbor's home and begged for shelter. Moved by the apparent grief of the samurai, they took him in and insisted he stay with them until the sharp edge of his sadness had blunted. This suited Kane well. While he stayed with his neighbors, the ghost of Ishi remained at bay.

A month passed. Kane continued to play the bereaved husband, and continued to sleep in his neighbor's house. But people began to notice that the grieving samurai would sometimes smile when in the company of Aiko. His friends and fellow warriors contrived to bring the two together as often as possible.

One day over tea, two of Kane's fellow samurai suggested that Kane marry Aiko. Hiding his triumphant grin in his cup, Kane haltingly asked them if they thought it would be proper, so soon after the passing of Ishi. Entirely proper, his friends assured him as a gust of wind slammed against the inn where they drank, causing the walls to rattle and shake. A stray breeze swept through the room with a sibilant whisper: "Vengeance. Vengeance." The breeze swirled through the steam rising from the teapot, shaping it into the broken form of a woman. The eyes of Kane's warrior friends glazed over. They both leapt to their feet, drawing their swords. Kane ducked and parried their blows, shouting: "What is wrong? Why are you attacking me?"

"Vengeance," hissed the rattling wind. "Vengeance," whispered the figure in the steam from the teapot, stretching its hand toward Kane's face. "Vengeance," chanted the two samurai together, their faces rigid, their bodies under the control of Ishi's ghost.

Kane upset the table, pouring hot tea over his friends. As he fled out the inn door, he heard swearing and gasping as the sting of the hot water pulled the warriors from their trance.

Kane did not pause until he reached a bend in the road. Only then did he look back. The giant, broken figure of Ishi towered over the inn, her crushed face and lolling eyeball leering at him mockingly. "Vengeance," she cried, stretching a hand caressingly toward him. Her bony arm grew longer and longer, until it reached the place where Kane was standing, transfixed.

At the last moment, Kane regained his senses and swung his sword at the hand, chopping it off. It fell to the ground at his feet and melted away. The towering ghost of Ishi laughed mockingly and vanished as Kane's friends came out the door of the inn. They remembered nothing of the ghost and were annoyed with their friend for spilling tea on them. Kane apologized many times before they would forgive him.

Shaken though he was by the reappearance of the ghost, Kane was still determined to woo and win the fair Aiko. He approached her father the next morning and was given permission to marry the daughter. Kane moved back to his home that afternoon and began preparing the house for his new bride. Then he grimly stayed awake all that night, expecting a visitation from the ghost. None came.

For a week Kane waited on edge for Ishi to appear, but her ghost had vanished. Relieved, Kane decided it was safe to bring Aiko and her family to see the home in which she would soon live. Proudly, he showed them each room in the house. Aiko was very much taken with the sleeping-room and lingered there while Kane took her parents out to the garden.

As he escorted Aiko's parents back into the house, he felt a hand on his arm, pulling him back into the garden. Kane turned and found himself face to face with a young, beautiful

Ishi, who kissed him and whispered a single word in his ear: "Vengeance." Laughing lightly, Ishi danced away, waving once toward the sleeping-room window. Still in shock from the encounter, Kane turned and saw Aiko silhouetted in the window, a look of bitter betrayal on her lovely face. Kane rushed indoors and tried to explain to his bride-to-be. The girl she had seen kiss him was a young cousin who was trying to make mischief, he told her. Aiko was placated, but from that time on did not trust Kane.

Fearing that Aiko might end the betrothal, Kane pressed forward with his suit, arranging for a grand engagement feast to prove his devotion to her. Friends, neighbors, and family came to the banquet hall and made merry over food and wine. Kane was pleased with the success of his feast. Aiko was smiling and warm, as she had not been since visiting his house. But when he looked up, he saw the beautiful young Ishi come into the room and stand demurely in the corner, facing him. Kane tried to distract Aiko so she would not notice Ishi, but Aiko was made suspicious by his sudden nervousness and she drew away from him.

Across the room, Ishi laughed softly and began to change, her beautiful body twisting and breaking before Kane's eyes, her face collapsing inward and bleeding, her black hair tangling with seaweed, her eyeball popping out of its socket.

"Vengeance," she whispered, reaching a hand toward Kane caressingly.

Kane shouted: "No! No! Leave here at once!"

Around him, Aiko, her parents, and their guests stared at Kane, puzzled by his behavior. None of them could see the ghost. Drawing his sword, Kane leapt over the table and attacked the ghost of Ishi, who laughed merrily and grew larger and larger before his eyes. Several of Kane's friends grabbed him and tried to wrestle the sword away, but he shook them all off. The ghost of Ishi drifted out the door and Kane followed her, shouting that she would haunt him no more. Ishi's ghost ran away from the banquet hall along the cliff path, the way she had once before walked with her husband. Kane ran after her, shouting and cursing. Suddenly, the ghost turned at the spot where Kane had pushed her over the cliff. She rose up and up, growing as tall as a tree, her face crushed and bloody, the eyeball swaying, and her shattered teeth gleaming in the moonlight.

"Vengeance!" she screamed, lunging at Kane. The samurai yelled in fear and dodged away from the ghost. His foot slipped on the loose earth at the edge of the cliff. He pinwheeled his arms for a moment, trying to regain his balance, and then fell backward over the edge.

Kane's samurai friends found his broken body on the beach, and they buried him beside Ishi. That same night, a terrible storm beat against the house where Kane had brought his new bride from Tokyo. A lightning bolt hit the roof, and the house burned to the ground. The neighbors claimed they could hear a voice in the foul wind that blew that night, saying one word, over and over: "Vengeance."

4

Llorona

RIVERSIDE

The feeling crept up on him slowly. At first, he did not even realize that he was shying away from shadows, hurrying to get home before dark, glancing over his shoulder as if he expected to see someone following him. When he did notice these things, he had no explanation for them. He was a retired widower. The days and nights loomed endlessly since he had grown too old to weave shawls, and they were lonely too, now that his wife was no longer there to share them. But his health was good, he had many friends, and his children all lived close to him. So why this feeling of impending doom?

He tried to laugh off the foreboding. After all, he had always had good luck. He was the one who found money on the street, the one who won free drinks at the local festivals, the one who always landed on his feet. Things had gone well for him all his life.

But he had noticed that lately his luck had changed. He began losing things—his glasses, his wallet, the keys to his house. He tripped over his own feet and fell up the stairs. He caught the influenza before anyone else. When he tried to hang a picture on his wall, the small mirror beside it fell and

21

broke into a million pieces. Seven years bad luck, he mused as he swept up the mess and threw away the shards of glass.

To make things worse, he started feeling as if something was dogging his steps. Every time he went out of his house, his neck prickled as if it sensed that someone was watching him. He kept turning around as he walked to see if anyone was following him, but no one was there. His eldest son teased him gently about his strange way of walking, saying that if he were not careful, people would think him senile.

"Something is coming for me," he told his old friend Lupe as they sat one evening playing checkers on his porch. "Something bad."

"Don't be crazy," Lupe replied. "You are just having some bad luck. Come to my house on Sunday night. We are having company over. You can relax, have a drink, and enjoy yourself. It will take your mind off your troubles."

He agreed reluctantly. Usually he liked visiting Lupe and his wife, but for some reason the thought of walking across town after dark made him nervous. His sleep was restless that night, broken by a soft wailing cry from outside his house that kept jerking him back to consciousness. It sounded like the cry of a baby, or perhaps a tomcat. But when he got up to investigate, there was nothing there.

He was heavy-eyed and irritable the next morning from lack of sleep. He grumbled to himself as he went to buy his weekly groceries. He had almost finished his shopping when he overheard a woman talking about the Llorona. He froze, his hand clutching an orange, and strained to hear what the woman was saying.

"There was a car accident last night," the woman told the

shopkeeper. "Several local boys were killed. I heard that the night before the accident, two of the boys saw the Llorona walking among the shadows, weeping for her lost children. And the next day, their car hit a palm tree right where they saw the Llorona."

The shopkeeper nodded her head. "Bad things always happen in the place where the Llorona appears."

He stood in silence, clutching the orange, remembering the wailing sound that kept waking him in the night. Had it been the Llorona, the Wailing Woman?

He had often heard the tale as a boy. The Llorona was a poor young girl who loved a rich nobleman, and together they had three children. The girl wished to marry the nobleman, but he refused her. He told her that he might have considered marrying her had she not borne the three out-of-wedlock children, which he considered a disgrace. The girl was determined to have the nobleman for her own, so she drowned her children to prove her love to him. But still he would not have her and married another. Mad with grief, the girl walked along the river, weeping and calling for her children. But they were gone. So she drowned herself. For her crime, her spirit was condemned to wander the waterways, weeping and searching for her children until the end of time. It was said that whenever the wailing woman appeared, someone would die.

He shuddered at the thought and hastily tucked the orange into his basket. After making his purchases, he hurried home. He put his groceries away and then spent some time searching his yard for signs of a stray cat or something that would explain the wailing noise that had disturbed him the night before. He found nothing.

LLORONA

He lay awake for a long while that night, straining to hear a wailing sound, but the only noise was the rustle of the wind in the palms outside his house. He drifted to sleep at last, and awoke with a pounding heart early on Sunday morning. Had he heard a cry? The sound came again, and he laughed aloud. It was the clink of the milk bottles being delivered next door. He turned over and slept.

Sunday evening found him huddled in a warm armchair, listening to Lupe Flores chatter with his guests. Many of them knew the boys who had been killed in the car accident, and the talk that night was of the Llorona. Someone pulled out a guitar and sang a song about the wailing woman that left many in tears.

It wasn't until the last guest had disappeared through the front door that he stirred from his chair. He shook the hands of Lupe and his wife and walked out into the dark night, the song about the Llorona echoing in his mind. He felt oddly at peace for the first time in weeks. No feeling of foreboding. No shying away from dark shadows.

He strolled along the street, thumping his cane against the pavement and humming the Llorona song. It was nearly midnight. The street was dark, but the sky was clear and the moon shimmered down upon the wrecked stone chimney of a small house that had burnt down a few weeks before. All that remained was the chimney and the blackened skeleton of the frame.

Among the dark shadows of the ruined windows, a white mist began to gather. It moved out into the yard and became the figure of a lovely young girl dressed all in white. Long, dark hair hung loose down her back. He stared at the girl, his heart thumping against his ribs. She moved gracefully, as if she were dancing, and began keeping pace with him along the road. He looked into her face, but she turned away from his gaze and began to weep. He suddenly felt very cold, and his hand trembled on top of the cane. The Llorona gave a moan of agony, and at the sound, a terrible pain shot through his left arm. Steel bands seemed to clamp around his chest. The cane slipped from his hand, and he crumpled into a heap on the ground.

A long while later, he heard voices above him. They sounded as if they were coming from far away. He opened his eyes for a moment and saw Lupe and his wife bending over him.

"Llorona," he said to his friend. "I saw the Llorona."

"Hush," Lupe answered. "We have called for an ambulance."

Behind Lupe's head, he saw a shimmering figure in white moving toward him. At first he thought it was the Llorona. Then, as the woman bent over him, he recognized the beautiful face of his wife. He smiled and took hold of her outstretched hand. She lifted him up, and his spirit parted easily from his pain-wracked body. Together they walked away, leaving Lupe and his wife to keep watch over his body until the ambulance came. From somewhere in the shadows, the Llorona gave a soft wail, but they were too involved with each other to pay attention.

5

Haunted House

I was working for a Fort Bragg lumber company back in those days. I was the general caretaker for a large number of company properties, both timber and ranch. It was a lonely job. I spent most days on horseback, riding various circuits that took me into the foothills to check on fences, make sure gates were kept closed, and see that the cattle on the ranches had access to watering holes. My closest friends were my horse, Buck, and a large guard dog inappropriately named Happy. Happy didn't like me much, which was high praise indeed considering that he alternated between despising and loathing the rest of the world. He would occasionally take a swipe at my hand and would growl if I patted him too often on the head; but he was company of a sort. No one ever bothered me when Happy was around.

I was courting a very nice young lady in Fort Bragg during my free time. She was a sweet girl. Happy had actually wagged his tail at her once and let her pat him on the head. A miracle! Lydia and I would go walking on Sunday afternoons after church, and her folks had invited me to dinner a few times. I was hankering to get me a wife and raise me a family, but Lydia was not the kind of girl to rush into that sort of thing, so my courtship was going more slowly than I would have liked. Still, I thought she would probably say yes when I proposed next week.

I was happily musing on my future with Lydia that Monday morning as Buck, Happy, and I set out. I was scheduled to ride the longest of my monthly circuits that week, so I had packed my camping gear and several days' worth of food. I was delayed quite a while with a downed fence at the first property, and it was late in the afternoon when I finished my chores at the second. I started riding out toward the old Phelps place and realized suddenly that it was going to have to be my last stop of the day. I shivered at the thought. I usually timed my visits to the Phelps place for around noon. It was an old, abandoned property with a monstrous, decrepit Victorian house that was supposed to be haunted. It should have been a good resting place for the local deer hunters, but they would not go near it. The few that tried came away before midnight with tales of ghostly thumping noises, gasps, moans, and a terrible wet bloodstain that appeared on the floor of the front porch and could not be wiped away.

"I'm not sure I want to camp there, Happy," I told my dog as I rode the overgrown trail that led to the abandoned house. Happy growled menacingly, which was his normal response to anything I said. Then he plunged into the undergrowth and disappeared after a rabbit. "Still," I continued, now addressing my horse, "if any of the fellows at work found out I camped outside the house, they would never let me hear the end of it. They're always daring me to spend the night there with the ghost of old man McInturf." Buck liked it when I spoke to him. He cocked his head and strutted a little bit, enjoying the nice weather and my company as much as I enjoyed his.

I pondered the story of the Phelps place as I rode toward the mansion in the quiet of the late afternoon. Phelps was an Englishman who had purchased land some 20 miles from the Mendocino coast in the 1880s. He had built a huge, fancy Victorian house all covered with gingerbread trimmings and surrounded by lovely gardens. He had fancy furnishings, including a piano and a huge library, shipped to him from England and brought in from the coast by wagon. Then, when everything was arranged to his liking, he had sent out party invitations to everyone within messenger range. And I mean everyone! Townsfolk, miners, schoolmarms, soldiers, ranchers, fishermen, loggers: Everyone was invited and everyone was looking forward to the housewarming party. It would be the biggest social event of the year, with music and dancing and lots of food.

Phelps roasted half a steer in a pit in the backyard. Sawhorse tables were set up with refreshments, and drinks were set out on the front porch. People arrived at the mansion in just about every type of conveyance known in the West. In buggies and wagons and pony carts, on horses and mules and donkeys, and even on foot, they came from miles around. Everyone who was anyone was there, and quite a number of people who might be considered nobodies, too. In fact, the only one missing was old man McInturf's son-in-law. They had had a terrible fight that afternoon, and the boy had stalked off in a rage, threatening to get even with the old man. Versions of the story were whispered all over the party as the guests mingled and chatted, danced, ate, drank, and danced some more.

Around midnight, the fiddlers took a recess to eat some dinner and rest. People broke up into small groups and roamed through the house and over the grounds. Old man McInturf stood on the front porch with some friends, chatting over the drinks table. Suddenly there came the thunder of hooves rushing up the lane toward the grand house. A cloaked figure on a white horse rode toward the lantern-lit porch. McInturf put down his drink. "That will be my son-in-law, George, come to the party at last," he told his friends as he went down the steps.

"George, is that you?" he called as the cloaked figure stopped his horse just outside the pool of lantern light. There was a sudden movement and then the loud reports of a gun firing twice. Old man McInturf staggered backward, shot in the throat and chest. The cloaked man wheeled his horse and fled down the lane as friends ran to the assistance of the old man.

"Did you see who it was?" Phelps shouted, running to the porch to help carry McInturf up the steps. No one had.

They laid McInturf down on the porch and tried to make him comfortable. He was bleeding heavily and they were afraid to move him much. There was some talk of fetching the doctor, who was attending a birth and so had not come to the party, but everyone knew it was too late for that. Too much blood was lost. It was pouring from the old man's wounds and had pooled underneath his head. McInturf coughed, once, twice; a hideous, gurgling, strangling sound that wrenched the hearts of all who heard it. Then he died.

HAUNTED HOUSE

McInturf's body was laid out on the sofa, and the once merry guests left in stricken silence. The servants came and wiped the red-brown bloodstain off the floorboards. The next day, a wagon was brought to the front of the house and McInturf's body was carried onto the porch. As the men stepped across the place where McInturf had died, blood began to pool around their boots, forming a wet stain in exactly the pattern that had been wiped up by the servants the night before. The men gasped in fear. One of them staggered and almost dropped the body. They hurriedly laid McInturf in the back of the wagon, and a pale Phelps ordered the servants to clean up the fresh bloodstain.

They never could keep that part of the porch clean. Every few weeks, the damp bloodstain would reappear. They tried repainting the porch a few times, but the bloodstain would always leak through.

Arrested for murder and imprisoned in the county jail, McInturf's son-in-law died of a blood clot in the brain. A few months later, one of Phelps's servants went mad after seeing a "terrible sight" that made his head feel like it was going to explode. Folks started saying the house was haunted by the ghost of McInturf, seeking revenge.

Phelps sold the house a few years later, and it changed hands a few times before being purchased by the lumber company. The house stood abandoned now and was slowly decaying. Hunters claimed that McInturf's ghost still haunted the place. They said that strange lights appeared in the windows and horrible sounds could be heard there after dark. Each time I visited the place (in broad daylight), I would look at the sagging front porch to see if there was a bloodstain there. But all the boards were weathered gray, just like the rest of the decaying house.

As I rode up the lane to the house, Happy burst out of the underbrush, darted through the skeletons of dead apple trees in the orchard, and danced around me and Buck, barking and capering madly. In the late afternoon light, I looked up at the decrepit mansion with its sagging porch, broken windows, and weathered gray warped siding. There were weeds everywhere in the overgrown yard, and the gate of the broken picket fence was hanging by one hinge. I led Buck to the well and gave him and Happy water to drink. I fed Buck some grain and tethered him loosely to a pine tree. Then I went to check the front porch. No bloodstain.

I made a fire on a bare patch in the front yard, and Happy and I ate some dinner. I wasn't too keen on the idea of sleeping in the house and had just about decided to bed down outside near Buck when I heard a rumble of thunder. Dusk was coming swiftly, brought on early by the dense clouds gathering overhead. The air was heavy and damp. That decided me. There was no way I was sleeping out in the rain with shelter close at hand. I put Buck into the remains of the old stable. There was a bit of roof left over one of the stalls, so I put him there and made him comfortable for the night. Then I took my sleeping roll, my rifle, and my lantern out of the saddlebag, and Happy and I made it into the house just as a vivid flash of lightning flashed overhead followed by a thunderclap that nearly burst my ears.

I lit my lantern and looked around. The house was dusty

and mostly bare. A few old pieces of furniture were scattered through the front rooms. I looked up the staircase, but decided I would rather stay close to the door in case I needed to make a fast exit, so I went down the hallway and found a few bedrooms in the back of the house. One room still had a door with a latch, and an old iron bedstead with rusty, but sturdy springs. I rolled my blanket out on the bed. Lightning flashed again. In the sudden light, I caught a comforting glimpse through the cracked glass of the window of Buck standing in the old stable. Then the heavens opened, and rain began pounding down on the house and yard.

I closed the door of the room, hoping that this would deter any ghost that might want to visit me, and lay down on the bed. Happy curled up on the floor and started snoring loudly. Even the heavy rain didn't drown him out, but I was used to it by now and so I fell asleep.

I'm not sure what woke me. Perhaps it was the silence. The rain had stopped, and Happy wasn't snoring. My arms were covered with goose bumps, and tiny hairs were standing straight up on my neck. Moonlight streamed through the broken window, lighting the room.

Beside the bed, Happy began to growl softly. Then I heard it. Thump. Thump. Thump. Someone was walking down the hall toward my room. Thump. Thump. Thump.

"Who's there?" I called, grabbing my rifle.

Happy was on his feet now. The hair on his back stood on end, and he was growling nonstop. Then I heard something cough, once, twice; a gurgling, strangling, wet sound. The door blew open. I gave a yelp of fright, aiming my gun at the doorway, but in the moonlight I could see that the hall was empty. Happy stopped growling. He prowled out into the hallway, sniffed around a bit, and then came back into the room. I got up shakily, closed the door, and bolted it firmly. I wasn't sure if the thumping sound and the coughing had been real, or part of a dream. But I wasn't taking any chances.

Happy curled up again and started snoring. I lay awake for a long time listening to the sound of the wind in the trees and watching the moonlight make strange shadows in the room. It was too wet to sleep on the ground outside, and Buck had the only dry spot in the stable. It made sense to stay in the house, but I desperately wanted to get out.

I fell into a restless sleep and dreamed I was at a fancy party in a miraculously restored Phelps mansion. I was pouring a drink for a beautiful girl who looked a lot like my Lydia when I heard Happy start to growl. I woke up, sweating, and grabbed my rifle. Thump. Thump. Thump. The footsteps were coming down the hall. The bolt flew back and the door burst open. A glowing figure staggered into the room, throat and chest bleeding heavily. It coughed once, twice; a terrible, wet sound full of death.

Happy took one look at the figure and leapt through the window, glass shattering everywhere. I followed him, ignoring the shards that tore at my hands and shoulders as I vaulted over the windowsill and out onto the tangle of wet grass underneath it. Happy disappeared into the woods. I ran into the stable and Buck greeted me with a surprised whinny. I flung myself down into the far corner of his stall, keeping Buck's large, warm body between me and the haunted house. I stayed there the rest of the night.

I waited until it was fully daylight before emerging from the stable. I had bandaged my hands roughly with some strips torn from my shirt. There was glass in some of the wounds, but I hadn't wanted to try to take it out with my knife while it was dark. I fed Buck, and then went into the house to get my bedroll, my rifle, and my lantern. As I stepped onto the porch, I looked down. A damp, red-brown bloodstain discolored the boards under my feet.

I ran into the house, snatched up my things, and left the property as fast as I could. There was no sign of Happy, and he did not answer when I whistled and called to him. I decided to return to Fort Bragg, have a doctor look at my hands, and finish my circuit later in the week. To my surprise, Lydia was waiting for me outside my house. She looked pale and upset. When she saw my bloodstained shirt and the rough bandages on my hands, she burst into tears. I took her in my arms and asked her what was wrong.

"Oh Tom, I have been so frightened," she gasped. "Happy came running into our house this morning, all covered with blood. I thought something had happened to you. Father rode out at once to look for you. I've been waiting here in case you came home."

I told her about seeing the ghost of McInturf and she scolded me soundly for sleeping in a haunted house. She made me promise never to do it again, which I was not reluctant to do. Then she insisted I have the doctor examine my hands. He dug several large glass shards out of my skin and he also ministered to Happy, which was brave of him.

Happy was never quite the same dog again. He was almost

friendly to most folks, and he adored Lydia, whom he seemed to think had rescued him from the ghost. Lydia insisted that we get married right away. She said it was obvious that anyone foolish enough to sleep in a haunted house, even during a thunderstorm, needed someone with sense to look after them. I didn't argue with her. And I switched circuits with another fellow at the lumber company, so I didn't have to go to the Phelps place again.

6

Innocenca's Revenge

The story began in the grand but lonely home of the village Don. He was a stern man of the old school, who had lost his wife many years ago. He was a tyrant to his servants, and to the locals, his manner was that of a judge—stern but fair to those who kept the law. The Don had one daughter, a beautiful girl named Innocenca upon whom he doted. She was the only person who could make the Don smile after the death of his wife. He considered his daughter the epitome of grace and beauty, and she was carefully kept from the company of the local children.

In the town lived a sea captain, a hearty red-faced man with a merry tongue. He had a handsome son who liked to sneak into the Don's garden and talk with Innocenca when she was walking alone or doing her embroidery among the flowers. The boy—Rodrigo—often journeyed with his father to far-flung places. When he returned, he would entertain the fair young daughter of the Don with tales of his exploits and of the many wondrous places to be found across the sea.

After one particularly long journey, Rodrigo returned home to discover that his young playmate had grown into a beautiful young woman. He swung himself up into the branches of the favorite tree he used to climb while telling her stories and paused to consider the matter. Aside from his father, Innocenca was the person he loved the most in the world. Now she was old enough to woo and win, if he dared.

Innocenca was sitting in the garden, working on a delicate piece of embroidery. She had not noticed the return of her old friend until he called to her. Upon hearing his voice, she dropped her embroidery and ran to the foot of the tree, smiling eagerly and holding out her hands. Rodrigo leapt gracefully to the ground and took her small, soft hands in his large rough ones. Something in his eyes told Innocenca what was in his heart before he spoke a word. She blushed as red as a rose and lowered her eyes while she told Rodrigo how happy she was to see him. Tucking her hand into the crook of his arm, Rodrigo walked her among the roses and spoke to her of love and many other things. By the time Rodrigo took his leave that night, they were betrothed, but secretly, for Innocenca was afraid that her father would not approve of the match.

For a month they met surreptitiously, aided by Innocenca's maid, Carlotta. Then Rodrigo got a position as first mate on a ship sailing to Brazil. A successful trip would earn him enough money to take a wife and build her a proper home. When he returned, he would brave the Don's wrath and seek Innocenca's hand in marriage. Each morning, Innocenca would look out over the sea and pray for the safety of her love, and each evening, she would sit opposite her father at the dinner table and plan how she would break the news of her betrothal to him when Rodrigo returned.

INNOCENCA'S REVENGE

Now Carlotta, Innocenca's maid, also loved Rodrigo, and she was jealous of his relationship with the Don's daughter. So she went to the Don secretly and told him about Rodrigo and her mistress. The Don was infuriated when he learned that his daughter was engaged to the simple son of a sea captain. He summoned his daughter and bitter words were exchanged. Finally, he forbade the match and ordered Innocenca locked into the tower room until she came to her senses. For many weeks she spoke to no one but her maid, Carlotta, and was given only bread to eat and water to drink. Still, she defied her father and waited for her love to come home.

Rodrigo returned, bearing with him a great fortune that he had amassed in Brazil. When he learned that Innocenca's father had forbidden the match, he went boldly to the Don's grand house and demanded to speak to its lord. The Don refused to see him, and the servants threw him out.

Desperate, Rodrigo sent a message to Carlotta, asking her to meet him in the village. When the maid arrived, he sent her back to the house with a letter for Innocenca, begging his love to run away with him. Carlotta solemnly swore to take the message to her mistress. Instead, she secretly burned the letter and told Innocenca that Rodrigo had betrayed her and was sailing back to Brazil to wed a woman he had met on his travels. Innocenca was heartbroken, and that night, she flung herself out of the tower window onto the rocks on the beach below.

In his letter Rodrigo had arranged to meet Innocenca on the beach at midnight. As he approached the meeting place, Rodrigo stumbled over the broken body of his love. With a moan of disbelief, he fell to his knees and gathered Innocenca into his arms.

Carlotta, prepared to lie about her mistress to the handsome young sailor, arrived on the beach moments after Rodrigo and realized that her mistress must have taken her own life in despair over her story. Carlotta was pleased. Now none stood between her and the handsome Rodrigo. Still, she was afraid that Rodrigo would blame her for the death of her mistress, so Carlotta thought up a lie to cover her evil deed. When Rodrigo looked up and saw the serving maid standing nearby, Carlotta fell to her knees, pretending to weep, and told him that the Don had found Rodrigo's letter to Innocenca and had burned it. Then he had locked Carlotta away from her mistress, forbidding her to serve the girl again. In her place the Don had sent a local girl from the village, one who envied the Don's daughter and wanted to make her unhappy. The girl had told Innocenca that Rodrigo had betrayed her, that he loved another girl, and was going back to Brazil to marry her.

"When I heard what the evil girl had done, I went to my mistress against the Don's orders, but I found her room empty. She must have believed the evil one's words and taken her own life!" Carlotta told Rodrigo.

Rodrigo hugged the body of his beloved to him and wept. Carlotta, afraid that Rodrigo would be blamed for the death of Innocenca, finally persuaded him to leave her body on the beach and to return to his home in the village.

In the morning Carlotta gave the alarm, telling the Don that Innocenca was missing from the tower room. After a short search, the Don's men found the girl's shattered body on the beach and brought her to the house.

The Don had his daughter laid out in state in the great hall of the house with candles surrounding her body. From morning until night, the whole household sat in mourning, grieving the death of the young Innocenca. Carlotta dressed herself in black and lay facedown beside her mistress's body, moaning and wailing in such an attitude of despair that the other servants took turns comforting her, never suspecting that it was an act. As for the Don, he spent hour after hour kneeling in his study, weeping for his daughter, and repenting of the way he had treated her in life.

That night, around midnight, a huge gust of wind burst through the front door, slamming it against the wall. Upon hearing the sound, the Don, who was praying alone in his study, came hurrying into the great hall and went to stand beside his daughter's coffin. From her place beside the body of her mistress, Carlotta sat up and stared toward the gaping black doorway. A small light appeared at the center of the door. It grew brighter, taller, wider. The spirit of Innocenca appeared within the light. She pointed accusingly at the maid Carlotta. Then she raised her arms. The wind whipped around her spectral form, flickering the candles that surrounded her dead body until a spark lit one of the large tapestries that decorated the hall. Suddenly, the great hall was in flames. The burning tapestry wrapped itself around Carlotta, who struggled in vain to free herself as she was engulfed by the fire.

Hearing the serving maid's screams, the servants rushed into the room carrying buckets of water, but the fire was already out of control. The fire rose up in a wall, trapping the Don beside his daughter's coffin. Suddenly, the spirit of Innocenca appeared before the encroaching flames with her hand out-stretched to her father. The Don took her hand and together they walked through the fire and out of the house. When she had taken her father to safety, Innocenca's ghost disappeared.

Down on the beach, the Don and his servants watched as the fire spread through the ground floor until it reached a secret magazine cache in the armory. The resulting explosion destroyed the house and much of the Don's wealth with it. The villagers came running to the scene of devastation, seek-ing ways to assist the Don and his household. Just for a moment, the Don came face to face with Rodrigo. In the light of the burning building, the two men stared at each other. Then the shoulders of the older man slumped in sudden despair. In one day the Don had lost his daughter, his home, and most of his fortune. He turned away and buried his face in his hands. Rodrigo hesitated for a moment and then placed a hand on the old man's shoulder. "Come, father," Rodrigo said. "Come and stay with me." Gently, Rodrigo led the Don away, and took him to live in his little house by the sea.

7

Lady in Lace

PEBBLE BEACH

By the time we had finished unpacking our suitcases, my wife had already grilled the staff about every ghost reported to reside in the area. Personally, I don't believe in ghosts, but my wife cannot get enough of them. She claims that she is psychic and tells me she can feel the spirits of the departed wherever she goes. That is fine with me. As long as she leaves me in peace to play golf and watch the latest on the sports networks, I don't care if she meets every ghost in Pebble Beach.

"The girl at the front desk says there is a ghost that walks along the Seventeen Mile Drive on foggy nights," Helen trilled from the bathroom, where she was refreshing her make-up. "She is called the Lady in Lace! Isn't that romantic? People say she is the ghost of Dona Maria del Carmen Barreto, the woman who used to own much of the land hereabouts. They think she returns to keep watch over her land."

Helen came out of the bathroom. "George, have you seen my shoes?"

"Over by the door, honey," I said, turning up the volume on the television. I had heard so many ghost stories over the years that I automatically tuned them out in favor of sports.

45

"There is another theory about the ghost," Helen said brightly, sitting down on the edge of the bed to put on her shoes. "People say the white, flowing lace gown that she wears resembles a wedding gown. So they think that she might be the ghost of a jilted bride who was left standing at the altar. The girl at the desk is in favor of this theory, because her boyfriend once saw the ghost, and he said she looked very sad and lonely, as if she were about to cry."

"That's nice, dear," I said automatically.

"The girl says the Lady in Lace can be seen near the Ghost Tree and at least one couple has claimed that she walked right past them while they were sitting on the rocks at Pescadero Point," Helen said, standing up and walking over to the table where we had piled all the tourist brochures. "So I thought we could take a ride up there and see what we could see. All right with you, George?"

"That's nice, dear," I repeated. At this juncture, my husbandly circuits kicked in and quickly replayed the conversation through my mind. Aghast, I turned down the volume on the television and looked at my wife. "I can't run around chasing ghosts! Fred and I are playing golf this afternoon," I said. "Which, may I remind you, was the whole point of this trip."

"I didn't mean right now, George," Helen said calmly. "Lynn and I are taking a tour this afternoon. I meant tonight after dinner. Once it gets dark. The girl at the desk said most of the ghost sightings take place at night."

I sighed with relief and settled back into the recliner. "As long as it isn't too late at night," I said. "I need to get a good night's sleep to stay sharp. I don't want Fred beating me on the links because I stayed up late chasing ghosts."

"We couldn't have that, now could we?" Helen said dryly. I ignored her sarcasm and turned up the volume on the television. Helen sighed and left the room to find Lynn.

I trounced Fred on the golf course that afternoon and was in high spirits after a pleasant dinner.

"So, when are we going ghost hunting?" I asked Helen after we said goodnight to Fred and Lynn.

"We can go tonight if you'd like," said Helen. "Although I wish it were foggy. Most of the ghost sightings along the Seventeen Mile Drive have taken place on dark, foggy nights."

"I wonder why?" I mused dryly. Helen ignored me.

"Still, we may get lucky," she said. "Come on! I have directions."

It was a beautiful, clear night. The moon rose high in the sky, its light shimmering on the ocean waves. I drove slowly, enjoying the beautiful scenery, while Helen kept a sharp lookout for any will-o-wisps wearing lace. She didn't see any. We spent nearly a half hour lurking near the Ghost Tree where the Lady in Lace was often seen, hoping for a sighting. We saw nothing.

Next, Helen said we had to visit Pescadero Point, where many folks had seen the ghost, including the couple who claimed the Lady in Lace had walked right past them while they were sitting on the rocks. Helen wanted us to repeat the couple's actions, hoping that the ghost might stroll past us, too. I didn't mind. It was a beautiful night and I was out with my beautiful wife. If watching for a ghost overlooking a romantic moonlit view was part of the deal, so be it.

We walked hand in hand down to the rocks overlooking the Pacific and sat down together, cuddling close and whispering to each other like a couple of teenagers. I sighed happily, watching the sparkling light dance upon the ocean waves. In the moonlight Helen looked just as young and beautiful as the day I married her.

Helen shivered suddenly under my arm. I squeezed her close and said: "Are you cold, honey? Do you want to go back to the hotel?"

"No, I'm fine. Just a sudden chill," she said. "A goose walked over my grave!"

I chuckled a little at the old expression, giving her a hug. Over her shoulder, I caught a glimpse of white. I stared at it. It moved closer, and I saw it was a woman, walking toward us. Her head was slightly bowed, and her face looked so sad that it nearly broke my heart. She was dressed in a long, flowing gown made out of lace.

I gasped. Helen turned in my arms, trying to see what had caught my attention. She stiffened and drew in a deep breath when she saw the woman in white.

"Now don't get excited," I murmured in Helen's ear. "It has to be a trick. We told the girl at the front desk that we were going to try to see the ghost at the point. She probably asked her friends to give us a ghostly experience."

Helen nodded, her eyes glued to the approaching figure. My skin broke out in goose bumps as I watched the Lady in Lace. I kept reminding myself that this was a trick. Around me the temperature dropped like a stone, and I shivered as the figure moved past the rocks where we were seated. She

LADY IN LACE

was so close that I could see the lace of her filmy dress swaying as she moved.

The woman did not utter a word, but I could hear the soft sound of her feet as she walked along. When the figure was exactly opposite my seat, an icy cold wave cut through me like a knife. With it came a feeling of mental agony such as I had never felt before. I gasped aloud.

The woman continued down toward the shore, and I saw that the bottom of her beautiful lace gown—it really could have been a bridal gown—was dragging in the dirt. She passed in front of a gnarled cypress tree, and I realized suddenly that I could see the tree right through her body! She seemed to glimmer in the moonlight, as ethereal as the dancing light on the ocean waves.

"Good lord," I whispered, shaken to the core. She disappeared from sight behind some rocks. I leapt up and ran after her, but when I reached the rocks there was nothing to see but empty beach. Helen hurried up behind me and caught my arm. She was pale and shaking.

"Let's get out of here," she said hoarsely. I nodded and half-pulled, half-carried her to the car. We drove in silence back to the hotel. I kept looking over at Helen, sitting quietly in the passenger seat. Tears were coursing down her cheeks. I started to ask her what was wrong, but she motioned me to silence. I helped her out of the car and kept my arm around her as we went up to our room. Helen broke away from me then and cast herself on the bed, weeping. I sat beside her, rubbing her back and wondering what to do. Finally, she sat up and wiped her eyes. "Oh George, she was so sad. So horribly sad. I could feel the pain coming off her in waves. And there was nothing I could do to comfort her."

I nodded. I was not psychic, like my wife, but I too had felt the sorrow from that white figure. And my hands shook every time I remembered seeing the tree right through her body and the glow about her that was brighter than the moonlight. I had never believed in ghosts, until now.

"I think I have had enough of ghosts for the time being," said Helen, taking a deep, calming breath. "Maybe tomorrow, Lynn and I can go shopping."

"That would probably be a good idea," I said.

I gave her a comforting hug and we went to bed.

8

Betrayed

HOLLYWOOD

It was a dark and stormy night, which, as everyone knows, is the very best time for telling ghost stories. Our three teenage grandchildren were visiting us for their spring break, and they had spent the day on a bus tour of Hollywood. Now, we all curled up in the living room around the fireplace with the lights turned out and listened to thunder rumbling outside.

"Tell us a ghost story, Grandpop," my grandson Bill said casually. "There must be ghosts in Hollywood."

"Dozens," I said, taking out my pipe. Abby, my wife of forty-five years, gave me a stern look—she hated it when I smoked in the house—but said nothing. I lit up and puffed for a bit, staring into the flames, letting the pounding rain, the flash of lightning, and the crash of thunder set the mood.

When the grandkids began stirring restlessly, I took the stem of the pipe out of my mouth and looked at them thoughtfully. The oldest, Clare, was nineteen and looked skeptical, which was appropriate. At the age of nineteen, I was skeptical about the whole world and wouldn't have believed in ghosts if one had walked right through my bedroom wall.

Becky was seventeen and had a rather nervous disposition. She looked terrified already, and I hadn't started talking yet. But she was eager, too, and I knew she would feel horribly cheated if I refused to tell them a ghost story. Billy was fifteen and absolutely bloodthirsty. Some of the urban legends I'd heard him swapping with his friends the last time we visited their home would make my ghost stories seem tame.

The final character in the scenario, my wife, Abby, sat rocking in her glider, knitting a scarf. If this makes her sound delightfully old-fashioned, let me rephrase the description. My still-blonde-and-determined-to-remain-so wife sat knitting a highly-modern, fluffy-looking scarf in electric colors, copied from a picture in the latest fashion magazine, which lay open by her side. She gave me an ironic stare. I smiled demurely back, which I knew would infuriate her, and began.

"I suppose I could tell you about the ghosts in the Hollywood Roosevelt Hotel. An old mirror there sometimes shows the reflection of Marilyn Monroe. And I have heard that the ghost of actor Montgomery Clift paces the hall outside Room 928, where he stayed for several months while he was making a film." I paused tantalizingly. Bill leaned forward, his eyes sparkling.

"Or perhaps I might begin with the ghost of Lon Chaney Sr., who played the original Phantom of the Opera, and who they say may still be seen running along the catwalks of Studio 28, wearing a dark cape," I continued.

Thunder rumbled, most appropriately, at that juncture. Becky gave a small shriek of terrified delight. Clare smirked and leaned against the back of her chair.

"Or maybe I could tell the story of the funeral procession of Bela Lugosi, the original Dracula. You know, the one where a ghost took control of the hearse on its way to the cemetery and forced the man at the wheel to drive down Hollywood Boulevard. Apparently, the ghost would not let go of the wheel until the driver crossed the intersection at Vine Street. People claimed it was the ghost of Bela Lugosi, making his way one last time down Hollywood Boulevard, as a final farewell gesture to his beloved town."

"His ghost took control of the car?" Bill repeated. "Nice!"

"Boring," Clare said. "I think I'll go upstairs and read for awhile."

"Go right ahead," I said amiably. "Meanwhile, I'll tell everyone else my favorite Hollywood ghost story."

Clare settled back into her chair. "I think I'll stay awhile longer," she said casually.

I suppressed a grin and told the children the following tale.

Around 1900, there was a lovely three-story inn in Beverly Glen where many people stayed overnight after going to the theater. A wealthy landowner was a frequent visitor, along with his very attractive wife. Sometimes the landowner's wife would come alone to stay at the inn. On one of these visits, she met a handsome young man. He was a bit of a dandy, always wearing outlandish clothes in his favorite color, yellow, but the wife liked him very much. Too much. The landowner's wife and the dandy began meeting regularly, and they always together stayed at the inn.

Then a friend of the family told the wealthy landowner about his wife's indiscreet behavior. The man was infuriated.

BETRAYED

He grabbed a scythe from the family farm and rode his horse into town, hoping to catch his wife and the dandy at the inn. The husband leapt off his horse, raced past the trembling innkeeper, and pounded up the stairs to the room he always occupied with his wife. Bursting through the door, he raised the scythe above his head and cut off the head of the dandy as his wife screamed and shrank away.

For this crime of passion, the wealthy landowner was executed, and his unfaithful wife inherited all his money. I don't know if she ever went back to the inn where her husband killed her lover, but her lover did return. They say that from that day to this, the dandy's ghost, dressed in glowing yellow with a fancy opera cape and a black bow tie around his headless neck, has often been seen standing beside the roadway, waiting for his love to return to him. And in the old roadhouse, the ghost of the husband can be heard bursting through the front door and pounding up the stairs to the room on the third floor where he was betrayed.

Thunder rumbled again, and everyone shivered. Clare finally spoke. "What happened to the inn?"

"It was turned into apartments," I said. "Haunted ones. Several of the tenants had mysterious encounters with the yellow dandy, and a couple living in the third floor room were terrified nightly by the sound of the betrayed husband running up the steps. The house is empty now."

"Well, that's enough ghosts for me," Abby said, casting off the final stitches on her scarf and standing up. "I'm going to bed."

The grandkids followed her out the door, leaving me alone in my chair, staring at the fire. I reflected for a moment on how lucky I was. I had a wonderful wife, great kids, and the best grandkids a man could hope for. I felt sorry for the betrayed husband, who had lost his wife and his life, and had never been able to rest in peace from that day to this. Yes, I was very lucky indeed. I snuffed out my pipe and went upstairs to bed.

9

Joaquin's Head

SAN FRANCISCO

Now, Joaquin Murietta was just about the most evil bandit in the West, at least according to some folks. Others claimed he was so kind he would give money to anyone that he found in need: the poor widow, the injured man who couldn't work, the orphan-child. Perhaps, like most folks in this wicked world, Joaquin was a mixture of things—a little bit bad and a little bit good.

He wasn't always a thief and a killer—oh no! When he was young, living in Mexico, Joaquin was a happy man with a sweetheart named Rosita and a dream of a good life. Then the local caballero decided he wanted the girl for himself. Joaquin and Rosita fled to the north rather than lose one another. They were secretly married and settled in California, living with Joaquin's older brother, Carlos, who was working a claim near Hangtown. The miners living nearby told them that it was illegal for Mexicans to pan for gold or hold a claim, but their words were shrugged off. Joaquin and Rosita planned to plant some corn and maybe have a small farm come the summer.

Their flagrant disregard for American laws outraged the miners. One night, a drunken mob led by a man named Bill Lang attacked the little family, shooting Carlos, and then ravishing and murdering Rosita while Joaquin was forced to watch. The mob bound the Mexican to a stake in the yard, where they beat him with a whip. With every stroke of the lash, Joaquin studied the faces around him, memorizing them. He strained angrily against his bonds, but finally he was overcome by his wounds and he slumped senseless against the post. The mob left him for dead. By the time a few sober citizens arrived the next day to help him, Joaquin had regained consciousness and fled.

A few months later a dark-bearded, longhaired stranger with cold black eyes set up a gambling establishment in Hangtown. It was a very popular place for drinking and losing money and gossiping. Soon enough, there was a lot to gossip about. It seemed that miners were going missing, one after another, and their bodies were turning up in unlikely places. All of them had their ears cut off.

At length, a few of the smarter folks realized that each of the dead miners had been a party to the slaying of Carlos and Rosita Murietta. There were thirty-one men in the mob that night, and fourteen were now dead. The other seventeen men scattered to the winds overnight. One by one, Joaquin Murietta found them all and killed them, cutting off their ears in revenge.

Eventually, a miner who had once had a claim near to the Murietta brothers came to Hangtown and recognized Joaquin as the owner of the gambling establishment. Murietta fled into the wilds and started to gather together a band of restless Mexicans. Soon he was the head of a mighty gang, riding a black stallion and robbing the Americans of their gold. He wore a black charro costume, rich with embroidery and silver buttons. His black sombrero had a gold hatband, and his stirrups were of pure silver. Dangling from his saddle was a string of dried ears.

There was one man of the mob whose ears were not on Joaquin's saddle. He was Bill Lang, the man who had led the mob to the Murietta house. Joaquin was saving that man for last, and Lang lived each day in fear and trembling. He could hardly eat and almost never slept. He tried to drown his fear in alcohol, but still he could never forget that his days were numbered. At last, the Mexican bandit rode up to Lang's house and rapped on his window. "Bill Lang, I am Joaquin Murietta. One day soon, I will come for your ears!" Bill Lang died instantly, his heart stopping in terror.

Together with his bandits, Joaquin robbed the miners of a million dollars in gold. Yet for all his ruthlessness, Joaquin was kind to his fellow Mexicans and would never turn down a friend in need. He gave his riches liberally to the poor and avenged those who were oppressed. In turn, they sheltered him from the law and called blessings down upon him.

Once, Joaquin and five of his men stopped by the camp of an American cattle driver and asked him for supper. The man obliged and invited them to spend the night at his camp. In the morning, he offered them breakfast, and as they were eating he addressed the young bandit by name. Joaquin tensed and one of his companions pulled a gun on the cattleman. "So you think you know him, do you?" asked the gunman.

"I knew him as soon as he rode in here," the cattleman said easily.

"Why did you not kill us then when we were sleeping?" Joaquin asked. "You could have collected the reward on me."

"As I see it, you've never done me any harm. I don't need the reward, and I don't like killing people," said the cattleman. Joaquin smiled and promised the man he would never be sorry. From that day forward, the cattleman never lost a head of cattle to any Mexican bandits.

Travel in the goldfields was made nearly impossible by the threat of Joaquin Murietta and his gang. A five thousand dollar reward was offered for the bandit, but he thought so little of his enemies that he rode into town one day and wrote a ten thousand dollar counteroffer on the sign. Finally, California's governor hired a group of rangers to track down and kill Joaquin. Led by a Captain Love, the rangers ambushed Joaquin and his men and shot the Mexican bandit and his horse to death. As he took his last breath, Joaquin looked into the eyes of the captain and said: "It is enough. The work is done." Then he crumpled to the ground, dead.

Captain Love decapitated the bandit and put his head in a jar filled with alcohol, which he paraded through the streets of San Francisco. The head was finally placed behind the bar of the Golden Nugget Saloon, where it leered at the folks who came there to drink.

A few months after his death, Joaquin's ghost appeared to one of the rangers, a man named Henderson, who had taken part in the ambush that killed him. Astride his coal-black stallion, still wearing the black charro costume rich with embroidery and silver buttons, the headless bandit loomed over the ranger as he was riding home to his ranch one night.

JOAQUIN'S HEAD

An unearthly cry rose from the stump of his neck: "I am Joaquin Murietta, whom you killed! Give me back my head!" The ranger fled in terror. For many nights following the incident, the ranger refused to go out after dark, because the voice of the ghost could be heard calling to him.

Out in the mountains, Joaquin's headless ghost continued to ride through the goldfields, terrorizing all who crossed his path with cries of: "Give me back my head!" Finally, the ghost located its head in the jar in San Francisco. On the anniversary of his death, at the stroke of midnight, the ghost made a spectacular appearance at the saloon, riding boldly through the door on his phantom steed and sweeping up to the bar. The ghost grabbed the jar containing the head and tried in vain to remove the lid. After prying futilely at the top, it disappeared in frustration, howling: "Give me back my head!" It was rumored that anyone observing the ghost was doomed to die in the next year, but none could verify the truth of the rumor. Still, every August 12, the saloon would empty before midnight, leaving the ghost of Joaquin alone with his pickled head.

The ghost's final visit to the saloon was on April 18, 1906, the day that the roof of the Golden Nugget caved in as a result of the mighty earthquake that destroyed much of San Francisco. During the quake, Joaquin's head tumbled to the floor and the jar broke open. Joaquin's ghost appeared instantly and swept down upon the still-rolling head, sweeping it up and onto its shoulders. "It is enough. The work is done," the phantom cried, and disappeared in a flash of light, to be seen no more.

10

Ghost Ship

MOJAVE DESERT

Somewhere between the land and the sky, through the blistering heat of the setting desert sun and the shifting, burning sands, sails a ship. Her sails are set to the wind, her rigging creaks and strains in the breeze, and the soft songs of her busy sailors drift through the twilight air. Eighty feet in length, her beams measure eighteen feet in breadth. Within her hold she carries a cargo of precious pearls. She sails straight into the sunset, turning neither to port nor starboard, her captain endlessly seeking to exit the inland sea that is drying up before his eyes. But it is too late. The ship is landlocked and cannot escape. She is doomed forever to sail on a sea long turned to dust and sand.

In 1612, the King of Spain commissioned the ill-fated ship, along with two others, to sail out of Acapulco in search of pearls. The expedition's divers were remarkably skilled in locating pearls, and the brass-studded chests that filled the ship's holds grew increasingly heavy with their finds. Their success led them farther and farther up the coast, but ill luck dogged their steps. The first ship hit a reef and sank beneath the waves near Isla Angel de Guardia. The captain of the second ship was

GHOST SHIP

ambushed and nearly murdered by hostile natives. He was forced to turn back, leaving only one ship, captained by Juan de Iturbe, to continue on the quest for pearls.

When the sailors sighted a narrow waterway with a southward current leading inland from the coast, Juan de Iturbe decided to follow it. At the time, people thought that a passageway existed between the Atlantic and Pacific Oceans, although no one had ever found it. Believing that he had discovered the fabled Straight of Anian, de Iturbe sailed down the passage until he came upon a vast inland sea. Excited by his find, he continued eastward to the far side, searching for a second passageway that would take them to the Atlantic. Alas, such a passageway did not exist, though they searched for many days.

As they explored the newly discovered sea, the sailors began to notice that the waters along the shoreline were receding at an alarming rate. Fearing that the narrow passageway would close behind them, de Iturbe turned the ship around and sailed westward as fast as the wind would take him. When the ship reached the western shores, they found the passageway blocked by a landslide.

Trapped, de Iturbe sailed the western shoreline, searching for another way out of the inland sea. But the ship ran aground against a sandbar hidden just below the receding water. The crew abandoned ship, taking all the treasure they could carry but forced to leave the bulk of it behind. De Iturbe and a few of his men made it back to the gulf and were rescued, but many of the sailors perished during the long trek to the coast.

The sea dried up around the trapped ship. Her useless white sails fluttered like wings in the breeze, her rigging creaked and strained. Soon her sails fell away. The boards warped and decayed until the thick ribbing stood alone like bleached trees. Chests of pearls lay buried within the rotting hold, covered by dirt, dust, and sand. Gradually, the ruins were engulfed by the sand dunes and seen no more.

The ghost ship was first seen by German prospectors crossing the desert on a search for silver. They had just made camp for the night and were settling down to eat when the ship sailed over the eastern horizon and passed by their camp on its spectral journey westward. It was surrounded by an eerie, otherworldly glow that lit up the darkening scenery around it. Her sails snapped in a stiff phantom breeze, and the rigging creaked and groaned as she moved through the phantom waters. The sound of long-dead sailors singing as they went about their work made the prospectors' hair stand on end. The startled men watched until the ship disappeared into the last rays of the setting sun. Though they watched late into the night, the phantom ship did not return.

She was seen again and again, sometimes sailing into the sunset and sometimes rising up in the moonlight, a rotted skeleton resting forlornly against a sandbank amid the receding waters of a long-dead sea. Many have searched in vain for the wreck. But it is said that one day the desert sands will shift, and the skeleton of the phantom ship will rise once again from her grave. The vast treasure she guards will finally make its way back into the hands of men. Only then will the ship's mission be accomplished and her journeying come to an end.

The Bells

SAN DIEGO

From the time she was a little girl, she remembered hearing the bells. She would awaken from a deep sleep to see the light of the full moon beaming through the window and on the breeze she would hear the tintinnabulation of bells. When she was old enough to speak, she asked her mother about it. Her mother crossed herself and told the child to hush.

"It is evil luck to speak of such things," her mother said, and would hear no more of the matter.

The child was puzzled. She had always enjoyed the ringing of the bells. The music filled her with a bubbling sort of joy that would make her laugh and dance over to the window. She would lean out into the moonlight and listen to the song of the bells. Someday, she would follow the sound to see where it led.

When she turned five, she asked her father about the bells. Her father told the child she was dreaming. "You are just like your grandfather. He also spoke of phantom bells that rang in the night."

"Did he ever follow them?" she asked her father. His smile faded.

"Just once, child. Just once," he said heavily. Her father would speak no more of the matter.

She often played with the other local children, and it was from them she learned of the buried treasure. One of the boys said that the gold had been taken by an evil priest whose duties for the church included counting the offerings and ringing the bells to summon people to Mass. The priest stole money out of the offerings to keep for himself. When he had filled a chest full of gold, he killed a man and buried him with the chest so the murdered man's ghost would guard it. Anyone who tried to dig for the treasure would be devoured by the skeleton of the murdered man.

The priest planned to return to Spain with his ill-gotten treasure, but he fell ill with a fever a week before his ship was scheduled to leave. On his deathbed, the priest repented of his crime. He swore to his confessor that his soul would not rest until he returned the gold to God. The priest died before he could reveal the place where the treasure was buried. As he gasped out his last breath, he said, "Follow the bells. They will lead you to the treasure."

The child believed her friend's story and was determined to follow the bells and find the treasure. When she repeated the story to her parents, her mother gasped in fear and her father frowned fiercely.

"No, my child," her father said. "The phantom bells you hear at night do not mark the location of buried treasure. That is just a made-up story. The sound you hear is that of the enchanted bells that mark the border between life and death. To those who hear such bells, the mysteries of both life and

THE BELLS

death may be revealed. But anyone who follows the music to its source will walk no more in life. Your grandfather used the knowledge the bells brought him to become a great healer. But one night, when the bells rang extra loud, he followed their enchanted sound to his doom. You must promise me that you will never follow the sound of the bells."

Reluctantly, she made the requested promise. She was an honest child, and so she kept her vow, although she often thought about the phantom bells. She was sure that her father was wrong about the bells. How could the sound of bells mark the border between life and death? It seemed much more likely to her that the sound of the bells was sent by the priest to show people the way to the buried treasure.

Then one day, her mother fell ill. Night after night, her father sat up with his wife, who was in terrible pain. The local doctor could not help her, but he spoke of a physician who might be able to cure the woman. The physician specialized in rare diseases and had healed many people whose lives might otherwise have been lost. It would cost more money than her father had to hire his services, but without his help, the local doctor feared her mother would die.

Frightened by the doctor's words, the child decided to find the buried treasure marked by the bells and give the money to the special doctor to make her mother well. She waited impatiently for the night of the full moon to come so she could follow the bells and dig up the gold.

When the night came, she listened for the bells. About midnight, she heard the sound of the phantom bells and immediately the child slipped out of bed and dressed herself for a journey. Then she crept out of the house and picked up a shovel that she had hidden in the shrubbery.

She followed the sound of the bells to the end of the lane, through the town, and out onto the open road. As she rounded a bend, the child heard the sudden thunder of horse's hooves, which muted the sound of the bells. A runaway wagon came screeching around the bend, headed straight toward her.

In that moment, the child saw the glowing white figure of a man standing between her and the runaway wagon. The sound of the bells grew louder. She could see them now, hanging in tall towers that marked the border of a far-away, misty land, and she knew then that her father's explanation of the bells had been the correct one. Around her, the roadway grew dim and the distant land came into focus. The border between life and death drew close to her. The glowing man was standing in front of the nearest bell-tower, only a few steps away. He beckoned to the child. In that instant, she realized that the man was her grandfather.

Her grandfather held out his hand. She hesitated for a fraction of a second, glancing from her grandfather's face to the runaway wagon speeding towards her. She knew she could not escape the doom that was before her. Reaching out, she took her grandfather's hand. There was a sudden flash of white light all around her. Then she and her grandfather stepped together over the border between life and death. Behind her, for the last time, she heard the musical ringing of the bells.

12

Jake's Camels

SIERRA NEVADA

I can't tell you how many times I came across old Jake tugging and pulling and cursing his mules as he went to and from his mining claim. He had the most ornery set of critters that ever roamed this earth. I told him to sell them and get himself a good horse.

Mind you, I like my mules. Stubborn as they can be, my mules have pulled me out of a couple of tricky spots over the years, including one day when I was hanging over an 800-foot drop with only the reins of my mule Samantha between me and certain death. But when a city slicker came to the gold-fields riding a beautiful black creature that was faster than a bolt of lightning, well . . . they don't call me Three-card Monty for nothing! That city slicker might have picked up a few gold nuggets out on his claim, but he should have stuck to panning and not gambling, because I got his horse!

I didn't want to part with my mules, though. People thought it was excessive, me keeping two mules and a horse, but I told them the black horse, Lightning, was for riding, not pulling wagons. So my mules, Samantha and Jude, spent their days eating the nice green grass in the small field behind my cabin, while Lightning and I worked my claim.

When I first got Lightning, I told Jake he could use my mules. In spite of the fact that he loathed the critters, Jake took splendid care of his own mules. But Jake had something else in mind.

"No, Monty, I would not use another mule again even if I had to carry every blasted nugget out on my own back!" Jake told me.

That night, Jake took off for San Francisco. When he left, he gave me his two mules, Buster and Bridget. Said he didn't need them anymore. Folks in town started calling me "the rajah" and bowing elaborately when they saw me, on account of me having four mules now, and a horse like Lightning.

"When are you getting an elephant, Rajah Monty?" the tavern owner called when I strolled in that evening.

"Next week, probably," I said. "It's still on order."

Everyone in the bar chuckled good-naturedly.

"So how do you like Buster and Bridget?" asked Fred Johnson, the man who ran the mercantile.

"They're not bad," I said, sitting down at his table after collecting a drink at the bar. "Apparently, all that ornery behavior was a personality conflict with old Jake, rather than just plain cussedness on the part of the mules."

"Really?" Fred asked, leaning forward with a gleam in his eye. "I've been hankering to get me a couple of mules. Are you willing to sell them?"

"I might be," I said casually, leaning back in my chair and putting on my three-card monte face.

JAKE'S CAMELS

We dickered for almost half an hour. In the end, Fred took home Buster and Bridget, and I took home approximately twice the money they were worth.

Jake came back from San Francisco two weeks later, leading three camels behind him. The whole town turned out to watch in amazement as the large, dirty, uncouth creatures walked down the main street behind Jake, who was wearing a huge smile. Now, I had thought that Buster and Bridget were just about the most cussed creatures on God's green earth— at least when they were around Jake—but these camels had them beat! The camels were meaner than a wildcat with a sore tail. When Jake stopped beside me, one of them took a bite out of his trousers.

"Get away from there, you crazy critter!" Jake said, swatting at its head fondly. It was clear to me that Jake was infatuated with the camels.

One of them turned a half-crazed eye on me and spat. Wiping my face as calmly as I could, I said, "What in blazes possessed you to buy camels?"

"The army is selling them, on account of the new continental railroad that President Lincoln approved," Jake told the small crowd that had gathered around. Everyone was standing as far away from the camels as they could and still hear what Jake was saying.

"I tell you, Monty, these camels can carry up to five hundred pounds of load each. That's twice as much as a pack mule! I call them Shadrack, Meshack, and Abednego," Jake cried enthusiastically, as Shadrack tried to kick me in the shin and Abednego coughed in Fred Johnson's face.

"Fancy that," I said, backing away cautiously.

"And one of the soldiers was telling me they can travel up to thirty miles a day, day in and day out. Not like a mule, no sir! A really good camel can go up to a hundred miles a day on level ground!"

"Do they understand English?" I asked doubtfully. "How do you get them to obey you?"

"One of the camel trainers from the Middle East taught me the basic commands," said Jake. "It's easy. Watch!"

Jake shouted some foreign words at the camels. They ignored him. Jake rattled the reins at them and shoved them from behind. Meshack gave a lazy yawn, and Abednego grabbed Jake's hat and started eating it. There were some sniggers from the crowd. Jake flushed and snapped his whip a few times. Shadrack snorted expressively, and Meshack kicked the tavern owner in the stomach. The camels put their heads together for a moment, and then all three started running at once, each in a different direction, dragging Jake along with them. Jake and his camels raced around a bend in the road and out of sight. We could still hear him cussing for a good long while after he disappeared from view.

Jake's camels were not popular with anyone in the area, but we got used to them. After awhile, folks wouldn't even blink when Jake and his camels strolled down the street. They might have been the most gol-durned stubborn animals ever created, but those camels sure could carry a heavy load, and they were real fast. Jake was always after me to race with him, but Lightning couldn't stand the camels. He went crazy every time they came too close.

The camels didn't like the mountains too much. They were desert creatures, and their feet would get torn up on the sharp mountain rocks. This worried Jake. He talked to me about the possibility of selling his claim and hauling freight down in the desert regions where his camels would be more comfortable.

Then, Jake and the camels disappeared for about a month. No one heard a word from them until Jake and his three camels rode right down the middle of the street one day with saddlebags full of gold nuggets. He had come to town to file a new claim. He'd discovered a new mine site that was brimming with gold.

Everyone in town got excited about the gold, but Jake wouldn't tell anyone where the new mine was located, even though folks bought him so many drinks that he couldn't see straight. I didn't like the way some of the new fellows who'd just come from back East were looking at Jake. One thin man with a mustache and cunning black eyes set too close together, Paul Adams by name, seemed to be paying close attention to every word he said. I told Jake to take care, but he just laughed at me and kept on drinking.

No one saw Jake alive after that night. A few days later, the bodies of Jake and his camel Shadrack were found in a remote area. They had been shot. Shadrack still had a torn piece of dark cloth caught in his teeth. There were signs of digging, but it was apparent that this place was not the location of Jake's new mine. The sheriff reckoned that Jake had been expecting people to follow him that night and so had deliberately gone to the wrong place. The murderer must have shot him and then discovered that he had been tricked.

Jake and his camel were buried together near his home, and life went on as usual. The sheriff tried to find out who the killer was, but other matters soon drove the mystery out of his mind. That burned me a little. Jake was my friend, and I wanted justice done. Every once in a while, I caught a glimpse of Meshack and Abednego roaming the hills, but they were always just a little too far away, and I never managed to catch them. Mind you, I didn't really want or need them. Out of respect for Jake, however, I thought someone should be caring for his camels.

Late one evening about a month after we buried Jake, me and a few friends were drinking and playing cards in the local tavern when we heard a terrified scream come from down the street. Everyone rushed to the door and looked out. A tall, thin chap came running around the bend in the road. I recognized Paul Adams at once. He was running as if his life depended on it, and kept looking over his shoulder. Then I heard a familiar voice, shouting in a foreign tongue. Around the bend came Jake, riding atop his camel, phantom saddlebags bulging with gold nuggets. Jake was shining with a brilliant white light, and Shadrack's eyes were glowing red. I could see right through them! Jake shouted again in the foreign tongue and whipped the camel to make it go faster. He was chasing Paul Adams with a maniacal gleam in his eyes.

The sheriff ran down the steps of the tavern and out into the street. With a scream of despair, Paul threw himself at the sheriff's feet, shouting: "I did it! I killed Jake! Save me!" I could see the tear in his trousers where Shadrack had bitten him just before he shot the camel.

The ghost of Jake thundered up on his camel and stopped

two feet away from the sheriff. They stared at each other for a long moment, man and ghost. The sheriff was trembling visibly, but his voice was calm when he said, "Thanks, Jake. I'll take it from here."

The shade of old Jake nodded. Shadrack spit expressively into the dirt beside Paul Adams. Then they disappeared.

The sheriff hauled Paul Adams over to the jail. The easterner wrote out a full confession of Jake's murder and begged to be put into the lock-up where it was safe. The rest of us were pretty shook up, too. My friends went into the tavern for another drink, but I paid my tab and walked home. On my way, I stopped by Jake's old cabin and stood awhile next to his grave. "I am sorry, Jake," I said aloud, feeling a bit foolish. "I've been trying to catch your camels, but they are still as ornery as ever. I'll keep trying."

As I spoke, the light in the clearing changed. I turned around. Jake and all three of his camels had appeared. Meshack and Abednego were strolling nonchalantly next to their phantom brother as if he had never left them. Jake led them into the yard, like I'd seen him do a hundred times or more. He beckoned to me, and I followed them up and up into the mountains to a remote place where a small mine had been dug out by hand.

"Well, there she be," Jake said, gesturing to the mine. "Good luck to you, Monty. Take care of my camels." He placed the reins in my hands. A chill passed through me as his ghostly hand touched mine.

"See you around, Jake," I said casually. My old friend gave me a jaunty wave. Then Jake and the phantom camel disappeared.

I stared for a long moment into the eyes of the remaining two camels, as the sun slowly rose over the horizon. Abednego coughed pointedly in my face and Meshack gave me a kick in the shins. It was practically a love tap, compared to the kick it had given the tavern owner a few months back.

"I don't know how I am going to reconcile you two with Lightning," I said finally. "Come on. Let's go home."

13

Voices of the Dead

It was a society marriage but a happy one. She married the heir to the Winchester Repeating Arms Company, which produced thousands of rifles for the Civil War. She was the belle of New Haven, until tragedy struck. Her little daughter, her Annie, died of an infant disease when only six months old.

She was stricken with grief, convinced that the death was a curse upon her family. For many months, she shunned society. Gradually, with the help of her William, she triumphed over her grief and resumed a normal life. But there were no other children to ease her loss.

Then William was stricken with tuberculosis. She watched him slip away from her, leaving her alone. She became the heir to the immense Winchester Repeating Arms Company fortune. To her it was bitter compensation compared with the loss of those she loved so dearly.

Inconsolable, and convinced that her family was cursed, she sought the counsel of a medium. The psychic confirmed her hypothesis. He contacted the spirit of her husband, who told his wife that he was being tormented by the tens of thousands who had lost their lives to the bullets of Winchester rifles. This was why first her baby and then her husband were taken from her.

Through the medium, she asked her husband what she should do to lift the curse and was told that these dead required a place to live. She must leave her home in the East and travel until she found a place where she could build a home for the troubled spirits. It would have to be a large home and it would need continuous updating, since every day more lives were lost to the bullets of Winchester rifles.

She set out immediately for the West, determined to follow her husband's instructions to the letter. At last, she purchased an eight-room house in San Jose and immediately began construction on a house for the dead. Feverishly, she added room after room to the house. Turrets, balconies, spires, and domes sprang up, creating a bizarre castle.

Hundreds of artisans and builders worked around the clock, every day of the year, to accommodate the Winchester ghosts. Yet still she felt them watching her, listening to her words, dogging her steps, and entering her dreams. She wanted to appease them. She needed to reach out to the dead, to hear their voices and to discover what it was they wished her to do. To accomplish this, she constructed a bell tower and an inner sanctum that she called the Blue Room. She had a servant toll the bell each night at midnight—the witching hour, when the spirits came to the house. Then she would enter the Blue Room, dressed in brocade robes, and she would listen to the voices of the dead. At two A.M. the bell would toll again, signifying the end of the night's consultation.

VOICES OF THE DEAD

She followed the spirits' instructions, building rooms and chimneys, secret passageways and towers, cabinets, doorways leading nowhere, balcony after balcony, and a staircase ending in the ceiling. Rooms were constructed, taken apart, and reconstructed. The house grew and grew, twisting and winding around in a labyrinth of corridors. Some halls were only two feet wide. Others had ceilings so low people had to stoop to go through them. Columns were inverted and installed upside-down. The door to one secret passage was at the back of the icebox. One staircase took forty-two two-inch steps to go up nine feet. The construction was endless, and the voices of the dead were never satisfied.

She quickly learned that the dead had a favorite number: thirteen. To please them, she constructed rooms with thirteen windows; she lined the drive with thirteen palm trees; she placed thirteen lights in the chandelier; she built staircases with thirteen steps.

She spared no expense. The interior rooms were luxurious, the gardens lavish and lush. She would play the piano with increasingly arthritic hands so the Winchester ghosts could dance. She gave up drinking after a ghostly handprint appeared in the wine cellar. She threw elaborate dinner parties for herself and the dead.

Still she could feel the eyes of the dead upon her. She grew frightened and reclusive, afraid that vengeful spirits would find her in her increasingly large mansion. She started sleeping each night in a different room and made the house even more mazelike and twisted to keep the dark forces at bay.

As the years went by, she shut out the rest of the world,

declining even to acknowledge a visit from President Theodore Roosevelt. Only the spiritualist Harry Houdini was allowed entry into the mansion. Still the work went on. A room was constructed with a window in the floor. Rooms were created within rooms. One door opened onto an eight-foot drop to the garden. Thirteen drainage holes were put into a kitchen sink.

In 1906, a massive earthquake shook the area. In moments, the seven-story mansion was reduced to four stories, and she was trapped for an hour by a blocked door. Terrified, believing that angry spirits had caused the quake because of her extravagance in constructing the front of the mansion, she stayed on a houseboat for a time and had the front thirty rooms sealed off. But the voices of the dead drew her back to her dwelling.

Death came to her in 1922. With her passing, the carpenters ceased all construction, leaving half-driven nails in the walls. She had continuously added to the house for thirty-eight years and spent $5.5 million to appease the dead. At the time of her death, the four-story house contained 160 rooms— including 40 bedrooms, 13 bathrooms, 6 kitchens, and 2 ballrooms. Within the house there were 10,000 windows, 950 doors, 47 fireplaces, 40 staircases (many leading nowhere), and 52 skylights.

When the safe she had used to store important documents was opened after her death, it contained the obituaries of her husband and daughter, along with locks of their hair, and her will, which was written in thirteen parts. A niece received all the furniture in the house, which took six and a half weeks to remove. Then the house was sold.

Today the Winchester Mystery House is a California Historical Landmark, and many visitors come to stroll through its tangled passageways and odd rooms. Some claimed to have seen the ghost of Sarah Winchester herself, haunting the house that once haunted her. Employees and tourists alike have reported many strange things happening at the house in the years following the death of Sarah Winchester—shattered windows, mysterious voices, cold spots. It appears that within the walls of this mansion, the voices of the dead live on.

14

The Lady of Mugu Rock

POINT MUGU STATE PARK

In the twilight between night and day, the ghost of a maiden sometimes appears above the crashing waves of the sea. The Lady of Mugu Rock's smile is sweet, but sad as she views the place where grief made her take her own life. At low tide, a rock emerges from the sea directly beneath the spot where the ghost is seen. This rock was once the maiden Hueneme. Beside it is another stone that was once her husband, who followed her into the ocean's depths rather than be parted from her.

Hueneme was the daughter of a great chief. She was merry and wise, beautiful and kind. Many were the warriors who came seeking her hand in marriage, but she loved none of them. Hueneme was content to live with her father until the day a strong and handsome warrior came to her village. Upon seeing him, she fell hopelessly in love. The warrior returned her affection and they were married. The happiness of the couple was so great that it was spoken of throughout the land.

But there was one who did not rejoice in the match, for she also loved the handsome warrior. This woman hated Hueneme and was determined to take her husband away. For months she studied the powers of darkness with an old sorcerer who lived in the mountains. Under his tutelage, she learned how to steal the warrior's love from Hueneme and make it her own.

The witch returned to the valley that she called home and set to work on her spell. When it was complete, she traveled to the village where Hueneme lived with her husband. As soon as he saw the witch, the warrior fell victim to her spell. Now blinded to the beauty and kindness of his wife, he followed the witch to her distant home and dwelt with her there for many days.

Hueneme was desperate. She neither knew where the witch had taken her husband, nor how, when she found him, to break the spell that bound him to the evil woman. She went to her father, the chief, to beg for his help.

Hueneme's father told her that her husband loved her still, in spite of the witch spell. In the face of her love, his spirit would not long be blinded by the witch's evil. She must find her husband and take him away with her.

Encouraged, Hueneme began searching for her husband. She traveled up and down the coast, asking at every village if anyone had seen the warrior and the witch woman. At last, she traced them to a distant valley. It was a foul place, the trees twisted, the air filled with the smell of rotting things. The witch's evil had tainted even the ground, so that the grass withered and died.

Hueneme found her husband living in the witch's house. She hid herself and waited for the evil woman to leave. Then she went to the house and spoke to the handsome warrior. He did not recognize her, but her voice touched a chord of memory. Deep in his heart, he remembered a happier time.

THE LADY OF MUGU ROCK

Hueneme persuaded the warrior to leave the witch's home and come with her. They crept away in secret. When the witch returned, she found her house empty.

Hueneme took her husband to Point Mugu on the coast. The warrior built a hut for them, and they lived there for many days. But the witch's spell still blinded Hueneme's husband. A taint lay across their happiness. At times, the warrior saw the witch's face rather than that of his beautiful wife. Sometimes he called Hueneme by the witch's name.

As time went on, Hueneme's hope turned to despair. Her husband would never again love her as he once had. The witch's spell could not be broken. Her father had been wrong. The power of love was not greater than evil. In the twilight between night and day, Hueneme walked into the crashing waves and was drowned.

Her husband, returning home from a successful hunt, saw too late his beloved wife slip beneath the waves. He called her name and ran to the water's edge, his heart breaking within him. But she was gone. Grieving, the warrior stepped into the sea and followed Hueneme one last time.

Upon seeing the sad fate of the once happy pair, the gods turned the bodies of Hueneme and her husband to stone and placed them near the shores of Point Mugu. They lie there to this day, united in death as they had once been in life.

They say the spirit of the witch also appears from time to time at low tide, hovering over Hueneme's rock. She is still trying to find a way to part the lovers, but she never succeeds.

15

The Lonely Grave

NEVADA CITY

The birth was not going well. Christopher did not need to see the look on the midwife's face to know that. The baby had come too early, much too early. The doctor was three days' hard ride away. They were lucky that the midwife had been home when the contractions started.

But that had been almost two days ago. Christopher didn't think that labor was supposed to take this long. His Maude was in terrible pain that did not stop between contractions. Every time Maude cried out, Christopher wanted to run to her, to make the pain stop. Finally the midwife threw him out of the house because his pacing was making her nervous and she needed to concentrate.

Christopher sat on the stoop, his head in his hands. The hours passed slowly. Finally, the midwife came out the front door and found him. Christopher read the news on her face before she said a word. The baby, his little son, was dead. And Maude was dying. The midwife sent him in to sit with her. There was nothing more she could do.

Maude lay very still on their small bed. Her tiny, premature

91

son was cradled in her arms. She barely had the strength to hold the baby but refused to let go.

"He looks just like you, Chris," she whispered weakly. "I want to name him David, after your father."

Christopher tried to smile. Maude did not seem to realize the baby was dead. It was probably better that way.

"David is a fine name," Christopher managed to speak without choking. Maude smiled and began crooning a lullaby to her dead baby, her voice growing fainter as death drew near. Christopher crouched beside her, his hand on her arm, too stricken to speak.

Then Maude looked at him out of her clear, gray eyes and said, "Chris, I want to be buried back East."

"Don't talk about that now," Christopher whispered, trying to hold back his tears.

"I want you to bury us beside my mother," Maude said. "Promise me, Chris."

The tears were streaming down Christopher's face. He nodded.

"I promise," he said.

Maude closed her eyes.

"I love you, you know," she said.

"I love you, too," Christopher answered, squeezing her arm.

Maude did not reply, and Christopher knew she was dead.

The midwife came into the room. She saw at a glance what had happened, and urged Christopher to go outside while she cleaned up mother and baby. Christopher saddled up his horse and rode into town to talk to the preacher about the funeral. He was too stunned to cry.

The whole town turned out for the funeral, which was held in the small church where Christopher and Maude were married. Christopher could not bear to be parted from Maude, so he arranged to have her buried beneath the single tall pine on a gently sloping knoll near their home on the hill.

"I'm sorry, Maude," he whispered to her headstone. "I just couldn't send you and David back East. Your family have each other back East, but you and David are all I have here with me."

Christopher visited the grave every night after finishing his shift in the mines. As the winter passed he grew thin and pale. He dreaded each day, knowing that Maude would not be there. He dreaded the nights even more, for darkness brought nightmares in which Maude appeared to him, gazing sorrowfully and looking toward the east. Christopher would awaken, racked with guilt, knowing that Maude was reproaching him for breaking his promise to bury her back East.

His neighbors grew worried about him, and sent the minister over to see what could be done to help him. Christopher found himself pouring out the whole story to the gentle, godly old man. The minister tried to reassure Christopher, telling him that Maude would understand and forgive him for keeping her grave near to him. But despite the minister's reassurances, the nightmares continued into the spring.

Each day, more and more fragrant wildflowers bloomed across the knoll. Christopher began bringing flowers to lay at the foot of the grave each night.

On the night of their wedding anniversary, Christopher threw himself across the flower-strewn grave, head buried in his arms as he tried to control his grief. As he lay there, the

THE LONELY GRAVE

stillness of the night seemed to deepen. A light breeze tousled his hair and swayed the branches of the pine tree.

At that moment, Christopher heard a soft voice crooning a lullaby. He started upright, searching about for Maude. He heard a gurgle from an infant, a happy sound of contentment. The breeze died away, and the branches of the pine tree stilled. Then a shining light seemed to descend from the dark sky and hover above him and the small grave under the tree. Christopher heard the singing again, and the happy laugh of a small child.

"Maude?" he asked. "Davy?"

The light caressed his face. For a moment, he felt a light weight on his lap, like the weight of a small child. Someone grabbed his thumb and gurgled happily. Someone else chuckled in his ear and tousled his hair, the way Maude used to. A kiss brushed his cheek. And then there was darkness.

Christopher sat still for a long time, a sense of peace filling him. For the first time he realized that Maude's body was gone, but her spirit was still with him. Wherever she and David were, they were happy.

Christopher rose.

"I miss you, Maude. And you, my little Davy," he told the gravestone.

That night Christopher dreamed of Maude and Davy. They were playing in a beautiful garden that was radiant with light. They looked up as he approached them, smiling and waving. Little Davy laughed up at his father and Maude took his hand.

"It is not your time yet, love. But we will see you by and by." She kissed him. Christopher woke up, tears streaming down his cheeks. He knew the nightmares were gone forever. He slept deeply that night for the first time since Maude's death. When he awoke, he realized he was looking forward to the new day.

PART TWO
Powers of Darkness and Light

16

The Hen and Her Chicks

CARMEL

It had been gray and cloudy all day. Night fell early. The Padre shook his head over the weather as he carefully lifted the hen and her seven chicks into the bag he had prepared for them. Old Eduardo over in Monterey was ill. When the Padre had seen his señora at Mass, he had told her that he would bring them over a hen and chicks to help tide them over while Eduardo could not work. The señora could sell the eggs from the hen, and some of the chicks would grow to be layers as well. The señora was very grateful, and thanked the Padre again and again.

He had meant to start out earlier in the day, but many small tasks had interrupted his plans. It was dusk when he set out on the path over Carmel Hill. Inside the sack, he could hear the little chicks cheeping as they cuddled close to their mother, frightened at first by the darkness of the sack and the motion. The hen clucked a few times and the chicks settled down. The Padre smiled to himself. Even after all the hard years of labor serving the people of Carmel, he still took time to enjoy the small miracles of life, such as the sound of a mother hen with her chicks.

THE HEN AND HER CHICKS

Darkness settled around him as he climbed the hill, but the Padre had walked this path a thousand times or more on his way to and from Monterey and his feet knew the way well. The wind sighed in the trees. He could hear the small sounds of the night creatures awakening and coming out to go about their business. An owl hooted once, twice. The air was warm and the Padre strode comfortably along in the moonless darkness.

Caught up in his thoughts, it took a few moments for the Padre to notice that the night noises had ceased. Something, or someone, was frightening the creatures. It was moving stealthily behind him. He tightened his grip on the sack and hurried faster. Bear, coyote, mountain lion? He wasn't sure what might be hunting him and he did not want to find out. The bushes near him rattled ominously. A dark figure rose up out of nowhere, and there was a sudden, blinding pain in his head. The sack fell from his hands as the Padre collapsed to the ground.

The robber cleaned the blood off the butt of his pistol and gathered up the frightened hen and her seven chicks. He bundled them into the sack, kicked aside the unconscious body of the Padre, and hurried down the path toward his home. A fine hen and a setting of chicks! A good haul, the man mused. And the Padre would probably wake up with a sick headache. No harm done.

As he reached his house, the robber swung the sack off his shoulder and opened it. It was empty! The robber stared into the sack, bewildered. He felt all the way to the bottom and then turned it inside out. Nothing! How could that be? He had put the hen and her chicks into the sack and held the opening closed all the way home. There did not seem to be a hole in the sack, but maybe part of the opening had slipped out of his grasp while he was walking and the hen and her chicks had slithered out.

Fuming at the inconvenience, the robber retraced his steps, searching along the path for the hen and her chicks. As he reached the top of the hill, the clouds parted. In the sudden brightness of the moonlight, he spied the unconscious body of the Padre lying beside the path. There was a great deal of blood coming from the head wound, he noticed uneasily. Then the robber heard a cheeping sound. Through the darkness, he could see the hen pecking at the ground. Her seven chicks were running around the Padre's body, scratching and poking about.

The robber hastily collected his booty, firmly closed the mouth of the sack, and carefully carried the sack home. In his mind, he kept seeing the blood all around the Padre's body. He had not been able to tell if the priest was breathing. But surely the blow had not been that hard. Just enough to knock him out!

Reaching the house, the robber opened the sack. It was empty. He stared into it blankly. It was impossible. He had carefully held the mouth of the sack closed the whole way home. He had felt the chicks rustling inside the sack. Now they were gone! Puzzlement gave way to fury. The robber stalked back up the trail, looking around for the hen and her chicks. There must be a hole in the bag, he fumed as he marched up the path.

As he reached the top, the robber could hear a scratch, scratch, scratching sound and the contented clucking of the mother hen. She was answered by the cheeping of seven baby chicks. Before him, next to the path, lay the Padre, his face and clothes covered with the blood from his head wound. He was surrounded by the hen and her chicks, industriously pecking away at the ground. Gingerly, the robber stepped around the Padre, trying to ignore a small voice in his head that insisted the holy man was dead. He collected the hen and her chicks and deposited them in the bag, after checking it thoroughly to make sure there were no holes through which they could slip out. Then he tossed the bag over his shoulder, keeping a firm grip on the neck, and hurried down the path. He was accompanied by the clucking and cheeping as he moved down the path. It grew fainter the farther downhill he went, but he could still feel the warmth of the hen and her chicks against his back. In his mind, he kept seeing the bloodstained face of the Padre. Murderer, his conscience accused him. You killed a holy man for a hen and a few chicks.

No! He wanted to scream the word aloud. He had only tapped the Padre on the head. The priest would awaken with a headache in no time. He hurried into his front yard and pulled the sack off his shoulder. He opened it carefully, and then dropped it to the ground. It was empty. The man felt his flesh creep. It was a judgment on him. He had killed a man of God, and this was his punishment.

He gave a cry of terror and ran into his house. He would not go back! Forget the hen and her chicks. He wanted to pretend the incident had never happened. He stood with his back pressed against the front door. In his mind, he saw the bloodstained body of the Padre lying beside the path, the hen and chicks scratching around it.

Chills ran through his body at the memory. The robber hurried to the hearth and built a fire to warm himself. Yet somehow, in spite of the warmth of the fire and the familiarity of his four walls, all he could see was the Padre, everywhere he looked. The crackling of the fire sounded to him like the clucking and scratching of the hen and her chicks.

He had to know! He had to see for himself what had happened to the Padre and to the hen and her chicks. Maybe then he could wipe the bloodstained face of the priest from his mind. He burst out his front door and practically ran up the path. As he approached the top of the hill, the robber heard a familiar scratch, scratch, scratching sound. A contented clucking was answered by the cheep of seven chicks. As he reached the top, the robber saw the hen and her chicks happily scratching the ground around the bloodstained body of the Padre.

The Padre lay so still in the moonlight. He was covered in blood from the wound on his head. The robber could not see any movement at all. He was sure now that the Padre wasn't breathing. I have killed a priest, he thought in horror. God would never forgive him for this crime.

The hen came over and pecked at his boot. The robber stared down at her. The sound of the hen and her chicks clucking and scratching grew louder and louder in his ears, until he could not stand the sound of it. He fumbled for his pistol, aimed it at the hen, and then turned it around and shot himself.

A villager on his way to Monterey found the bodies a few minutes later. There was nothing he could do for the man who had been shot, so he left the body beside the clucking, scratching chickens and carried the injured Padre down the hill. While the doctor was patching up the priest, several men went back for the body of the robber. When they arrived at the top of the hill, the hen and her chicks were gone.

The robber was given a Christian burial and the patched-up Padre prayed at the graveside for his eternal soul. The hen and her chicks were never found, so the Padre sent another hen with her brood over to sick old Eduardo and his wife. They say that on dark nights, folks walking over Carmel Hill can still hear the phantom clucking and scratching of the hen and her chicks.

Juan Stops Flirting

LOS ANGELES

Maria was the mother of a large family. Six children had she, and she was very proud of them all. Five of her boys and girls had good jobs, were married, and had made her a grandmother. But oh, that Juan! He was her youngest boy, and such a wild one! He had a good job, mind you, and made a lot of money. But he refused to settle down! He was always drinking and carousing around the city and flirting, flirting, flirting with the pretty girls. Never serious about any of them! Maria was in despair. She had lectured him and pleaded with him, but Juan would not listen.

"I am old, my son!" Maria exclaimed one day when Juan came to visit after work. "I would like to hold your children in my arms before I die."

"Nonsense, Mother! You will outlive all of us," Juan said cheerfully, waltzing her around the kitchen and giving her a kiss on the cheek. "Now I must be off. There's a new girl serving drinks at the tavern, and she's a pretty one! Maybe a new daughter for you?" Juan winked at his mother.

"That is what you said last week," Maria called out the

105

window as her son sauntered away. "And the week before that, and the week before that, and the week before that!"

Juan waved merrily at his mother and headed to the bar for a drink and a bit of flirting with the new girl. Not too much, mind you. He was getting tired of pretty girls showing up at his apartment, weeping all over his carpet and claiming he had led them on. Of course, the weepers were much better than the ones who threw things. And even the throwers were better than the ones who showed up with their parents in tow. He'd had to skip town a few times to avoid them.

It wasn't, Juan mused, that he didn't want to get married. He just wasn't ready to settle down yet. There were so many lovely girls out there. Why settle for just one?

Juan took a seat at the bar and had a few drinks. The pretty server made him laugh a few times, and he thought about asking her to have dinner with him. Then the door opened, and a beautiful woman dressed all in black came into the tavern. She wore a fancy black hat with veiling that softened and blurred her face a bit. Every man in the room was staring at her, unable to look away. She just seethed with sensuality. Juan decided then and there that he was going to ask her out.

The woman sat down at a table in the corner. She was immediately surrounded by men wanting to buy her a drink. She fended them off with a wave of her black-gloved hand. Her voice, Juan noted, was deep and sultry. He decided to bide his time. He would approach her after she left the bar. He kept drinking and flirting with the server, watching the woman out of the corner of his eye. She had two drinks and then got

JUAN STOPS FLIRTING

up to leave. The eyes of every man in the room remained glued to her until the door closed behind her.

Juan was ready. He had already paid for his drinks. Now he slipped out the back door and around the alleyway to the front of the tavern. The woman was walking slowly up the street. Every move she made breathed sensuality. Juan's heart was beating fast with excitement as he hurried after her.

"Señorita! Wait, please," Juan called. The woman stopped and turned to face him. The veil obscured her features, and Juan wondered eagerly what she would look like when he drew close enough to see behind the veil.

"You wish to speak to me, Señor?" the woman asked in her deep, sultry voice, the sound of which sent thrills down Juan's spine. This was a woman worth having, he thought as he stopped at her side.

"I was wondering if you would like to have dinner with me?" Juan asked. To his embarrassment, his voice cracked like it had not done since his early teens. He sounded like an eager schoolboy. All of his polish seemed to melt away before this woman in black. He looked hard into her face, trying to see her features behind the thin veil, but they were blurred. He caught a glimpse of a rounded cheek and the glow of a dark eye.

"Why would I have dinner with you? You spent all evening flirting with the server," the woman said coolly.

Juan flushed. "We are just friends," he stammered.

"Does the girl think you are just friends?" asked the woman.

"She means nothing to me," Juan said desperately. "Please, Señorita, please have dinner with me."

"And if I have dinner with you, what then?" asked the woman. "Will you leave me in the morning, like you have so many others?"

Her sultry voice burned like fire through Juan. His body was aflame with desire. In that moment, Juan would have said anything, done anything to persuade the woman to have dinner with him.

"I would never leave you, Señorita," Juan swore rashly.

"Never is a long time," the woman said softly. There was an edge to her voice that grated a bit on Juan's inflamed senses. She sounded smug, as if she had been waiting for just such a promise. "Are you prepared to put that in writing?" the woman added.

A sudden breeze blew around Juan's cheek and the woman's veil fluttered a moment. Underneath the veil, Juan caught a glimpse of fathomless black eyes lit by tiny red flames, of pointed white teeth almost hidden by bloodred lips. For the first time, he noticed that her hat was perched upon her head strangely, as if it was covering two small horns. The woman pulled her veil back into place with one hand. In the other hand, she now held a large book.

The fire in Juan's blood turned to ice. He backed away suddenly, staring at the veiled face of the woman, and then at the black book she carried. What had she asked him to do?

"If you sign the book, *I* will have dinner with you," the woman in black said enticingly. But her voice had lost its charm. All Juan could think of was the glimpse he had caught of black eyes lit with red flame, of pointed white teeth almost hidden behind a bloodred mouth. Juan let out a terrified shriek and ran down the street. Behind him, he heard the woman laughing. A mocking voice called: "What? You do not wish to flirt with *me*, Juan?"

Juan ran for his life. He had never told the woman—or whatever it was—his name.

His parents' house was closer than his own, and it was full of religious icons. He would, Juan felt, be safe there. He skidded in the door, almost knocking his mother down in his haste to reach shelter.

"Juan, what is it? What is wrong?" Maria asked, leading her shaking son into the kitchen. In a voice hoarse with fear, Juan told Maria about the woman in black and her book.

"I think it was the devil," Juan concluded, a shudder passing through his body. "I think the devil was trying to make me sign over my soul."

Maria nodded her head but very wisely said nothing, although she wondered if this demonic encounter was the answer to her prayers for her son. She offered Juan some tea and then tucked him into the spare bedroom for the night.

Maria did not see much of her youngest son for the next several months. Then one evening, he called and invited himself to dinner. He brought with him a very pretty, very religious girl whom he introduced to both his parents. They had, Juan explained, met at church. Maria was impressed. Never before had Juan brought a girl home to meet them, and in the past he had refused to attend church. After dinner, Juan announced his engagement to Therese. His father gave a hearty shout of congratulations and shook his son's hand. Over his father's shoulder, Juan met his mother's eyes and grinned ruefully. Maria grinned back. Then she stepped forward to hug her youngest son and his bride-to-be. Juan had stopped flirting at last!

18

The Princess's Curse

DEATH VALLEY NATIONAL PARK

Many a long year ago, there lived a Queen who ruled over a lovely valley hemmed in by steep mountains. Her kingdom was a peaceful one and her subjects thrived under her rule. One summer, the Queen fell in love with a brave and strong warrior. The couple was married within a fortnight of their first meeting.

The Queen's happiness spread to her people and her land. The fertile valley seemed to glow with joy so that even the goods traded with other kingdoms had a bit of that radiance and were valued more highly than those from other lands.

To the Queen's delight, a daughter was born to herself and her consort. The infant had the beautiful large eyes of a doe and a smile that touched the deepest places within the soul. She was beloved by all. The people of the valley counted themselves privileged if they so much as caught a glimpse of the little princess.

When she was still quite small, the little princess fell ill with a fever. Her parents sat with her night and day for a week before her fever broke. The day the medicine man declared the princess out of danger, the Queen wept aloud with joy and relief. The little princess was slow to grow strong again. She no longer ran and played in the beautiful gardens and pathways of the valley but was content to stay at home and embroider or practice on the little pipe her father had given her as a gift. The Queen was alarmed by the change in her daughter and insisted that the child take numerous herbs and potions brewed by the medicine man. But none of them restored the little princess's strength. She remained a fragile, delicate jewel whom the people treasured even more than before.

When the princess was sixteen, her father was killed in a hunting accident. The Queen was distraught and locked herself away in her rooms for many days. When she finally emerged, she was changed. The sweet openness of her manner was gone, replaced by a coldness that the princess had never seen before. Outwardly, things went on normally in the valley kingdom. However, the glow of happiness had left the Queen and her people, never to return.

The grief of having lost not one, but both of her parents made the princess more fragile than ever. The cooks made every delicacy they could think of to tempt her royal appetite, but she ate sparingly and grew pale and sickly.

The princess watched with alarm as her mother's gaze turned outward, toward other lands, as if she were seeking something to fill the void left by the death of her husband. And finally the Queen did find a new project to engage her interest. The Aztecs, to the south, had built great palaces and created many treasures. The Queen decided that she would surpass them all.

That very day, the Queen commissioned all the best builders and workers of timber and stone in the valley to build her a palace such as had never been seen before. Soon the valley was filled with the crash of falling trees. The beautiful pathways became ugly dirt roads down which large stones and timber were dragged. Foundations were laid for a huge, magnificent palace. The Queen was pleased and smiled for the first time since her consort's death.

As days and weeks turned to months, the Queen grew impatient. The palace was taking shape too slowly. She commanded more of her people to help with the work, carrying stones, dragging timbers, and aiding the skilled workers. All other work in the valley ground to a halt. The palace was the only thing that occupied the waking moments of the Queen and her people. The princess went to her mother and protested the treatment of the people. The Queen shouted at her daughter and commanded her never to speak disparagingly of the palace project again within her hearing. From thenceforth, the princess was no longer allowed to enter her mother's presence without being directly summoned by the Queen.

The Queen grew angry because the project slowed at mealtime. She forced the people to work in shifts and begrudged the time that the men took to hunt and the women took to cook, insisting that they continue working on the new palace by torchlight far into the night. And still, the work was too slow for the Queen. She took to strolling among the workers, a whip cradled in her beautiful hands, and she lashed the backs of any man or woman who was not working with the industry she required.

The princess was enraged by the Queen's treatment of the people. Defying her mother's command, she boldly came before the Queen and berated her for her cruelty. The Queen struck the princess across the face and had her locked in her room until she learned to respect the royal decrees of her parent. The princess remained a prisoner for many days with only stale bread to eat and water to drink, until the Queen at long last relented and released her. The Queen's blow and the lack of food had taken its toll on the delicate health of the princess. She lay ill for many days following her release. The Queen took no notice of the princess's health and refused to send for the medicine man or allow anyone to nurse her.

Close to a year after the start of her project, the Queen began having the same dream each night. In the dream, she lay on her bed, dying of fever, her palace half-completed. She was all alone, with none to comfort her. The Queen was frightened by her dream. She could not, would not die before her palace was finished. She ordered all the children of her people to work with their parents on the palace, even those who had just learned to walk.

At this last monstrosity, the princess rebelled. Rising from her sickbed, she came before the Queen, begging her to have mercy on the children. Infuriated, the Queen had the princess dragged out to the work site and forced her to work side by side with the people. The Queen stood nearby, watching as the men, women, and children toiled in the hot summer sun. Anyone who slowed down felt the touch of her whip across his or her back. One warrior tried to take the heavy burden from the princess, whose fever had returned and was climbing steadily. The Queen had the warrior beheaded where he stood, and then she beat her daughter with the whip until the princess fell to the ground, the load of stones tumbling from her arms.

The princess lay trembling on the ground, her back a mass of welts and blood. Drawing on the last of her strength, the girl rose shakily to her feet and confronted her mother. "A curse I lay upon you," she cried, "and upon this valley. May it wither and die as the love for your people has withered and died away, never to return. Your palace, your people, and your kingdom will perish ere your palace is complete."

She fell to her knees as she proclaimed the last words and then pitched forward and lay dead at her mother's feet. The Queen stared down at the lifeless form of her daughter. Slowly the whip fell from her hand. Above her, the heat from the sun trebled as her daughter's curse took immediate effect. A rebellious murmuring was heard from the workers. They considered royalty sacred and so had obeyed their Queen without question. But matters grew confused when the sacred destroyed the sacred.

The heat from the sun blasted down upon the work site as the Queen knelt and gathered the body of her daughter into her arms. She did not seem to notice that one by one, her workers were abandoning the site. Those men whose strength had not yet been defeated by the project packed up their families at once and left the valley. But many of the people were too weak to flee the cursed valley. Day after day, as the Queen sat alone in her house weeping over the body of her daughter, the people watched the valley die around them. The water dried up, the trees and grass withered, and the animals disappeared. The very

THE PRINCESS'S CURSE

old and the very young perished first, followed by the rest. At last, only the Queen remained, lying on her bed, dying of fever. She dragged herself out to her half-completed palace, and lay with the terrible, hot sun beating down upon her until she breathed her last.

To this day, the half-completed palace of Death Valley may be seen in the shimmering mirage that sometimes appears on the horizon in the heat of the burning sun.

19

The Corpse Walker

SIERRA NEVADA

My Uncle Liang went to make his fortune in the goldfields of the Sierra Nevada. He had been restless ever since the death of his wife, my Aunt Bik. Theirs had been an arranged marriage, but the love that had arisen between them was deep as the sea. Even though I was quite small when Aunt Bik died, I remembered how her house seemed to sing with happiness.

I watched while Uncle Liang packed his things. He told me stories of the old days, when he and Aunt Bik lived in China. His voice trembled a bit when he said his wife's name. I wondered if a woman would ever love me as much as my aunt had loved my uncle. I was not sure if I was comfortable with that idea. After all, look how terribly unhappy my uncle was after she died. Perhaps it was better to be comfortably married, like my parents. I shook my head and decided not to worry about it. Marriage was still a long way off. I said this aloud to Uncle Liang, and he smiled. "Not too far off now, Shen. I hope you will find happiness as great as that I had with Bik." He patted me on the head and went to speak to my father.

Upon his departure, Uncle Liang begged my parents for one promise. If anything should happen to him, his last wish was to be buried beside his beloved wife. My father solemnly assured him that we would honor his request. Satisfied, he bowed to each of us and left for the goldfields.

We did not hear from my uncle again for many months. Then one day a man came to our door. He wore the rough clothes of a miner, and his face was grim and sad. Uncle Liang had fallen to his death, he told us, away up in the mountains. The trail where he was found was steep and narrow, and so they had buried him there rather than risk another life by bringing him down the mountain. My father and mother exchanged glances. I knew they were remembering the promise made to my uncle. My father valued his honor above all things. I knew he would do whatever it took to bring my uncle's body home, no matter what the cost to himself or his family. For my father, it was a matter of honor.

At my father's request, the miner made a map showing us where they had buried my uncle. Then he departed.

"What will we do, Father?" I asked, even though I knew what his response would be.

"I made a promise to your uncle that he would be buried beside his wife. I will not dishonor him or myself by breaking that promise," my father said. "I will go and bring him down."

Father left the next morning and was gone for three days. He returned without the body of my uncle. The path on which my uncle had met his fate was even more treacherous than the miner had described. It was so narrow in places that a man had to inch along sideways, holding on to the cliff face, to reach the ground on the other side. My father could not carry my uncle out.

"Then we must find a Walker," my mother said firmly. My father blanched at the thought. Then he nodded his head slowly and told my mother he would make inquiries.

I was curious. I had never before heard of a Walker. When Father left the house, I asked my mother what a Walker was.

"Back in China, some of the holy monks are called Corpse Walkers," my mother said. "When a person dies, the body they leave behind becomes an empty shell. That is why we bury them so quickly, so no evil spirit can take over the body. But sometimes, like in your uncle's situation, it is necessary to move a body that is nearly unreachable. When this happens, one of the monks places part of his spirit into the body and walks it to a place where it can be safely transported. Your father is going to find a Corpse Walker to bring out your uncle's body."

I shivered. It sounded horrible.

Father came back late that night. He had found a Corpse Walker. Both repulsed and curious, I asked Father if I could accompany them on their mission to retrieve my uncle's body.

"It is no place for a child," my father said firmly. But I was his only son, and he indulged almost all my whims. With a little persistence, I persuaded him that I should come along.

We traveled for a day and a half, up into the steepest parts of the Sierra Nevada. Finally, the trail became so narrow that we abandoned the cart. The path was only wide enough for one person to walk at a time. We climbed single file for nearly a half hour. Finally, we reached the ledge that Father had

THE CORPSE WALKER

described. I inched across it sideways with my heels out over a very high drop, my hands clutching the rocks in front of me for dear life. My heart pounded and my legs trembled so much I thought I would fall. Pride alone kept my mouth shut and forced me past the narrow place. I didn't look down.

My uncle was buried a few yards away from the ledge. Together, my father and the monk dug up his body. He had already begun to decay, and the smell was terrible. They laid his body on the ground. Then the monk closed his eyes for a moment. I got the impression that he was focusing his mind on my uncle's body. Suddenly, the body twitched. I jumped backward in shock. The eyes opened and my uncle slowly rose to his feet. Loose earth dropped from his clothing, but he did not brush it away as a living man would. I felt my flesh creep at the sight. There was nothing alive about him. His eyes were open, but there was no spirit looking out of them. His body did not stand erect as it had in life. It sagged a bit to one side. Probably where his bones had broken in the fall, I surmised.

The monk opened his eyes and motioned to my father and me to precede him back over the ledge and down the path to the cart. Father went first, carefully inching along the narrow ledge. I followed, keeping my eyes on the cliff face until I was safely past the drop. Then I looked back. The monk was moving carefully along the narrow ledge, his face pressed against the rock in front of him. Behind him, sliding along just as carefully, came my uncle's body. Clods of earth broke away from his clothing and fell down, down, down into the canyon below.

The monk stepped onto firm ground, followed by my uncle's corpse. It trailed the monk down the path, hopping stiffly behind him. I kept turning around to gaze at the body in horrified fascination. Once I bumped into my father in front of me. He told me, rather sharply, to behave myself. After that, I looked only ahead until we reached the place where we had left the cart.

The monk walked directly over to the cart and my uncle's body followed him. At a gesture from the monk, the body climbed into the cart and lay down. The monk closed his eyes for a moment. My uncle's body shuddered, and then was still. The monk opened his eyes and clutched at the side of the cart for support. It had taken a great deal out of him to bring my uncle's corpse so far. My father was ready with a flask of tea and some food. When the monk had eaten and drunk, we drove down the mountain with my uncle's body. We buried Uncle Liang next to Aunt Bik, just as we promised.

20

The Serpent

LAKE TAHOE

Well now, after the war I settled myself down on the west shore of Lake Tahoe. Built a cabin, bought me a hunting rifle, and got the pick of the litter from a neighbor's setter dog. Figured I would retire and spend my days hunting and fishing.

Me and Jake, my setter, would roam up and down the shores of the lake and then wander back into the hills, hunting and sometimes just walking about enjoying each other's company. My Sally, may she rest in peace, was a bit of a chatterbox, and I cherished the silence, since I reckon I'd heard enough conversation to last me a couple of lifetimes. Jake didn't say much, him being a dog, but we managed quite well together. He liked to sit in the boat and watch the water while I fished. I won't say he held the net for me every time I landed a big one, but he always passed it to me, which amounted to the same thing.

I didn't have any near neighbors, so the only socializing I got was when I went into town. I'd been in my new home for a few months when I heard a few folks in the local grocery store talking about a serpent. Now, "serpent" is an old-fashioned sort of word. Most people hereabout call the slithery critters "snakes." I was intrigued and did some eavesdropping to find out what they were talking about. After hearing only a few sentences, I hurried away, made my purchases, and left the store. As soon as I was out of earshot, I bent double laughing until I cried. They were talking about a sea serpent! A sea serpent in Lake Tahoe! Jake bounced about barking excitedly. He wanted to be in on the joke, I guess. I kept chuckling to myself all the way home. These old-timers sure did have good imaginations.

The summer passed and autumn blazed across the lake country. The days and nights were chilly indeed, but that didn't stop Jake and me from hunting and fishing every chance we got. Early one morning, when the sun's light was glowing through the mist that rose off the lake, Jake and I set out to hunt for grouse. I'd spotted some near one of the creeks that fed into the lake and was aiming to bring back a dozen before the day was through.

As I combed the brush, I heard a loud crashing sound coming from the mouth of a nearby canyon. Jake barked sharply as the ground started to shake. Suddenly, a flock of quail burst forth, flying right past my face, nearly blinding me with their feathers. They were followed by more rabbits than I could count. The bunnies were hopping just about as fast as I'd ever seen, rushing by me without taking any notice of my hunting dog or my gun. Jake and I were so startled by the strange migration that we stood stock-still and just watched. The rabbits were soon joined by a pack of coyotes. I always thought coyotes ate rabbits, but these fellows were too busy running to bother.

I was becoming uncomfortable with the scene before me. These animals were frightened. You could feel the fear coming off of them in waves. A herd of deer had joined the throng, and they were stumbling over the rabbits and each other in their determination to exit the canyon. Jake's hair was standing on end and his tail was tucked under his body. It would not take much more to spook my setter, and the sight of two huge bears loping through the mouth of the canyon did the trick. Jake gave a yelp of terror and fled with the other animals. The bears passed by so close to me that I could have reached out and touched them if I dared. But from the look in their dark eyes, the very last thing I wanted to do was get between them and their destination.

My arms were covered in goose bumps, which was strange because I was sweating fiercely. It occurred to me that a thing that even bears feared was something I did not want to meet. Almost without conscious volition, my feet carried me over to the nearest spruce tree and I found myself climbing up as high as I could go. The thickness of the branches covered my hiding spot. I watched as the last of the strange migration petered out, leaving an eerie quiet behind. No birds chirping, no rustle of small animals moving in the underbrush. There was just the cool touch of the wind and the silence.

Then I heard it. The scraping sound of something very large sliding—or should I say slithering—over rocks and stone, tree roots and other debris littering the floor of the canyon. Scrape. Swish. Slither.

An ancient terror filled me. I could feel my hair stand on end, and my clothes were soaked with sweat. My arms were

THE SERPENT

shaking so hard I could barely cling to the tree branches. The sound grew nearer, and then I saw a wide, flat head with pitiless dark eyes appear in the mouth of the canyon. It was a serpent. The largest serpent I had ever seen. It was thicker than a sequoia and longer than a house. It was mostly black, with some dull orange markings along its side. I held my breath as it slowly slithered out of the canyon. It stopped for just a moment and raised its wide head. The cold black eyes looked this way and that, searching for something. I hoped it wasn't me. My body had frozen in terror. I did not make a sound. Then the head lowered again and the serpent undulated down the creek, heading toward the lake.

Cautiously, very cautiously, I turned and watched it slither along, passing right over small saplings and dislodging very large rocks as it passed. A foolish quail that had not fled with its companions erupted suddenly from a bush. With a lazy snap of its giant mouth, the serpent swallowed it right out of the air. Then it slid into the lake and began swimming toward the far end. I watched its graceful movements through the water until it submerged. I didn't come down from the tree for a very long time.

It was more than an hour later when I heard a familiar whine from the foot of the tree. Jake sat beneath me and wagged his tail apologetically. My mind came back from whatever faraway place the fear had taken me, and I slowly let go of the tree limb and slid down to join my dog. Jake thrust his nose into my hand, for his comfort as well as my own.

I cleared my throat a couple of times and said, "Well then, Jake, what do you think about moving somewhere a little less hazardous to our health?"

Jake whined again, which I took as agreement. Within a week, I had sold my cabin, and Jake and I went to live near the coast. Apart from the occasional sea lion that tried to take up residence on my fishing boat, we lived a peaceful and happy life. We never went back to Lake Tahoe again.

21

The Devil and the Prisoner

LOS ANGELES

Now, Antonio was a merry soul who liked nothing better than to drink the night away with his friends. They would laugh and tell jokes and drink toasts until none of them could see straight and walking became a bit of a problem. Antonio was a bachelor, and he liked being a bachelor, but his parents were growing old and kept begging him to get married. So Antonio finally married the prettiest, richest girl in Los Angeles, much to the delight of his parents.

You would think such a marriage would be a success. But no! Unfortunately for Antonio, he had forgotten to look behind the pretty face before he proposed, and so had found himself married to a shrewish woman who nagged him from dawn until dusk. At least once a week, his new bride complained to her father about the laziness of the man he had chosen as a son-in-law. Then Antonio would be lectured by his father-in-law, berated by his mother-in-law, and threatened with violence by his brother-in-law if he did not treat his sister right. His only refuge from such a horrible existence was in the bottle. At the end of these weekly torture sessions, Antonio would go out drinking.

131

Antonio's friends all felt sorry for him. They all knew his wife and felt that he had a good excuse for his wild habits. They took turns buying him drinks and listening sympathetically to his predicament. He had a rather good imitation of his father-in-law that he could be persuaded to do after five or six drinks. It always made his friends laugh.

One evening, after a particularly long lecture from his father-in-law, Antonio's wife threatened to leave him. "One can only hope," Antonio muttered aloud. That did it! His wife was furious. She stomped out of the house to find her brother, who was always threatening to pummel Antonio. Fearing for his health, Antonio fled to the local tavern in search of solace.

After many drinks with his friends, Antonio stood up on a chair and described what he would do to his brother-in-law if he got the chance. One of his particularly spectacular gestures overbalanced his chair and Antonio crashed to the floor. As it turned out, this was a good thing, since the brother-in-law in question came through the front door just at that moment. Quick as a wink, Antonio crawled away under the tables and lit out the window. Unfortunately, he landed on the local constable, who happened to be talking to the owner of the tavern at that moment.

Well, the constable did not take too kindly to being knocked off his feet by a drunken man. He frog-marched Antonio to the jail and locked him up tight. At first, Antonio thought this might be a blessing in disguise, as it made him inaccessible to his brother-in-law and his wife might be persuaded to make good on her threat to leave him. Then he realized that if his father, who had a heart condition, ever found out that his only son was in jail, it would be the death of him.

Antonio remembered a spell that one of his friends had taught him that would summon the devil if ever one needed his aid. So Antonio staggered around in a circle three times (bumping at least once into the little cot they had left in his cell) and called out to the devil to come to him. At once, a voice hailed Antonio from outside. He felt his way carefully over to the window and peered out through the bars. A tall, dark, whiskered chap with pointy ears and a devilish smile sat atop a black horse. Small horns peeked out of his well-combed hair.

"So, you wish to make a pact with the devil, do you?" the man asked.

"Yes I do," Antonio slurred. "You wouldn't want to take my wife, would you?"

"No sir!" the devil said promptly. "I know your wife! She is a shrew without equal. Offer me something else."

Mildly disappointed, Antonio thought for awhile and then offered the devil his best horse in exchange for his freedom.

"Done!" said the devil. "Just stick your head through these bars and I will pull you out."

This sounded sensible to Antonio. He pushed his head obligingly through the bars of the window. At first, they seemed hard and unyielding. Then he felt the devil tug on his ears and the bars began to bend like rubber. His head was nearly through when he heard his wife's voice shouting his name from up the street.

"Holy Mary, Mother of God!" Antonio swore. The devil yelped as if he had been stung when he heard the name of the Virgin Mary. He let go of Antonio's ears. With a popping sound, the devil and the black horse disappeared, leaving

THE DEVIL AND THE PRISONER

Antonio with his head firmly wedged between the bars of the window. And that was how his wife and brother-in-law found him. The jailer was summoned, and he was forced to saw the bars clean through to get him out.

As they started for home, Antonio's wife began berating him for his drinking, for getting himself thrown into jail, and for getting his head stuck trying to escape so she wouldn't know he had been imprisoned. This was the last straw! Antonio stopped right in the middle of the road and began yelling at his wife and brother-in-law.

"Escape? Of course I was trying to escape," Antonio shouted, "but not to fool you! It was for the sake of my good parents. With my father's heart condition, I was afraid the news might kill him, so I made a deal with the devil. I asked the devil to help me get out of prison in exchange for you. And do you know what? The devil would not take you! He said you were a shrew without equal, and he was right! If it wasn't for my parents' health, I would have been happy to stay in prison for the rest of my life if it meant never having to see you again!"

Leaving his wife and brother-in-law staring after him in shock, Antonio stalked home and went to bed with a hangover. The next morning, his wife brought him breakfast in bed. He could tell from her eyes that she had been weeping.

"We looked at the bars again this morning," his wife said, avoiding his eyes. "There was no way you could have gotten caught between them—they were too close together—unless the devil did help you. Did he really call me a shrew without equal?" Her voice caught on the last word, and she began to weep.

Antonio sat up cautiously. His head was pounding. He wanted to be quietly sick and then go back to sleep. But he sensed that he was at a turning point in his marriage.

"Yes, that is what he said," Antonio answered his wife.

She nodded her head sadly. "My brother said the same thing last night. He said I treated you shamefully, and that if his wife ever complained about him the way I complained about you, that he would go out drinking every night and never come home."

She set the tray down on the side table and looked Antonio in the eyes.

"I am sorry," she said. "I will try to do better." She left the room and closed the door behind her.

Much to Antonio's surprise, his wife kept her word. She would never be the ideal wife, but she stopped complaining about him to her family, and she tried helping around the house more and nagging less. With a more peaceful house to come home to, Antonio found less need to spend evenings at the tavern, which made his wife happier. And once his wife had a few children, she became too busy to nag at him, which made Antonio happier. They never again spoke about Antonio's pact with the devil.

The Guardian

YOSEMITE NATIONAL PARK

I watch over this land from high above. I take delight in the song of the birds, the smell of green things growing, the sound of the wind in the trees. It is a good land. Its beauty fills my heart with joy. The people who live in the valley have given me a name—Tisayac. This pleases me, for it means they sense my presence and feel at home in this valley. I have guarded the people of this land from afar for many a year. They are a good people, strong and kind.

Thus it was with great interest that I saw a great chief arise from among the valley folk. Tutokanula was his name. Handsome was he, brave and kind, and well-loved. His intelligence greatly enhanced the lot of his people.

Many days, I would come down from my musings among the clouds to watch this man, who went further than any other leader of men to save crops and preserve game so that his people might have an easier winter. His wisdom and his kindness touched my heart. Often I would dream of him when the night wind sang through the trees and night flowers perfumed the air.

In the early evening one summer, when the twilight was upon the fields and valleys, I saw Tutokanula hunting in the woods near my resting place. I moved closer, studying the frown of concentration on his face, the strength of his arms. Suddenly, he looked up and saw me! I was startled and shrank back among the bushes. Our eyes met. I felt my cheeks flush as his dark eyes took in my fair skin, blue eyes, and golden hair. There was no hiding who I was, for none of the people in this land looked as I did. He recognized me at once and gasped the name his people had given me: "Tisayac."

I stood up and answered him: "Tutokanula." He came to me, swift and straight. My heart beat faster when I saw the look on his face. Suddenly, I felt shy. When he opened his arms to me, I fled, lifting up into the sky and hiding myself in the clouds.

Overcome as I was by the rush of feeling the chief had engendered in my heart, I took myself off to the heavens to seek wisdom and peace. Time does not exist there, and so I did not realize how long I had been away until I came again to my valley and found it a place of ruin and despair. I was horrified. What had happened to my valley?

I drifted invisibly among the people, trying to discover the cause of the disaster that lay before me. Soon enough I understood it. Tutokanula had forgotten his people, had left them to fend for themselves without the benefit of his great wisdom, and had spent many days and nights searching and longing for me. Oh, what had I done? In my despair, I knelt upon a mighty dome of rock and prayed with all my heart that the Great Spirit would undo this wrong, would restore to this land the virtue that had been lost.

THE GUARDIAN

A gentle wind touched my cheek. I looked up into the heavens and saw that the Great Spirit had taken pity on the plight of my people. Stooping down from on high, he spread his hands over the valley. The green of new life poured forth over the land; trees blossomed, flowers bloomed, birds sang. Then he struck a mighty blow against the mountains, and they broke apart, leaving a pathway for the melting snow to flow through. The water swirled and washed down upon the land, spilling over rocks, pooling into a lake, and then wandering afar to spread life to other places. In the valley, the corn grew tall again, and the people came back to their home. Somehow, they knew it was I who had asked the Great Spirit for this miracle, and they called the rock where I had knelt to pray "Tisayac."

There was one face missing from among them. I searched in vain for a glimpse of Tutokanula. The beauty of the valley paled for me, and I sought refuge in the clouds, my heart sore with longing for the kind chief who loved me. At last, my ear caught the sound of a knife chiseling away at stone from the top of one of the mountains. I was curious and floated over to see what was happening. And there he was, my Tutokanula! He had returned to the valley. He was busy carving something into the stone. I wanted to fly to him at once but was afraid to startle him, lest he fall.

I was curious to know what had caused him to make a carving on the mountaintop. I drifted once again among the people, seeking an answer to the puzzle. I heard them speak of their chief. His love for Tisayac, for me, was as strong as ever. He had come to the valley because he had heard that I had returned, and he was carving his likeness into the stone so his people would remember him when he departed from this earth. My heart was troubled at these words. Was he ill? Had some sickness taken his strength? Was he dying of love . . . for me?

When the carving was finished, Tutokanula sat down at the foot of the beautiful Bridal Veil Falls the Great Spirit had created. He was older now, with some gray in his hair, and his face was weary with longing and unrest. He loved me still, his people said, and I loved him too, so dearly. I drifted into the spray of the falls, watching him. He was ready to depart from his people, from his valley. Dared I hope that he would come with me? My heart was pounding in my breast, but I had to know. I moved forward through the falling water and made myself visible. The radiance surrounding me was reflected in the light of the rainbow from the waterfall. He looked up suddenly and saw me. Our eyes met, and this time, when I saw the look of love in his face, I did not flee. I spoke his name and held out my arms to him. Tutokanula sprang to his feet with a cry of such joy that it brought tears to my eyes. He leapt into the falls and took me into his arms at last. The light from my spirit spread over him. For a moment, there were two rainbows arching over the water. Then I drew him with me, up and up into the clouds and away as the sun sank over Yosemite.

23

May I Carry Your Sack?

SAN FRANCISCO

I think tales of ghosts, haunts, spooks, and bogeymen of all sorts are complete nonsense. No right-thinking, logical man like me could possibly believe in them. So a few weeks after my twelfth birthday, when folks living in my neighborhood started talking about a bogeyman that was haunting the streets late at night, I ignored them. I was old enough to know better. Unfortunately, my mother was one of the most gullible—I mean susceptible—recipients of such tales (plus she was the neighborhood gossip), so I heard them all.

One woman claimed that an eight-foot, headless skeleton had accosted her and its head had chased her all the way home. An old man said that a tiny child with demonic red eyes had whispered to him in the dark as he passed the place where it stood. Apparently, the child had removed its head at one point in the conversation, causing much agitation to the old man telling the story. One girl saw a headless soldier, and another was accompanied home by the head of a black dog. That was enough for me. I told my mother I was going to study with a friend and left the house.

My friend Doug lived about a ten-minute walk downhill from our house. When I arrived, I told him about our local bogeymen, and we laughed until our sides ached. Then we took out our homework and got busy studying until dinner.

After dinner, Doug's father challenged me to a game of chess. Doug is no good at chess, but his father is a champion. I liked to play him every chance I got. I always lose, but I am getting better with each game. Someday I plan to wipe up the floor with him.

It was getting late, and my mother called twice to find out when I was coming home. She was really worried about me. She didn't want me walking alone after dark, not with a bogeyman roaming loose in the city. She wanted to drive down to the house and pick me up. How embarrassing. I told her "no way" and said I would come home as soon as the game was done. "And don't wait up!" I added for emphasis.

"Mothers!" I said to Doug. He rolled his eyes in agreement.

I was after 11:00 P.M. when we finished the game. (I lost, but only just!) I put on my jacket and Doug walked me to the door.

"Don't let any bogeymen get you," he told me with a grin.

"Oooh! I am so scared!" I replied.

"Maybe you should call me to let me know you got home safe," Doug said mockingly. I punched him lightly on the arm, and he laughed as he shut the door.

The only trouble with visiting Doug's house is the walk home. It is straight uphill, and somehow my legs never got used to the climb. The night was dark. Clouds filled the sky, shutting out the moon and the stars. Even the street lamps seemed dim and didn't light the road as well as they should. If I were a superstitious man, which I am not, I would think it was not a

MAY I CARRY YOUR SACK?

good night to be walking alone. However, I reminded myself, I laugh at stories of skeletons, children who remove their heads, and bogeymen of all sorts.

Climbing the hill ahead of me was the stooped figure of an old woman. She looked familiar. Old Sara, I think she was called. She lived mostly on charity, and my family tried to help her out whenever we could. My mother would not be happy to hear that old Sara was out roaming the streets on such a chilly night. I hurried to catch up with her.

As usual, she wore a hodgepodge of clothes, and had wrapped a tattered shawl around her head, totally obscuring her face. She carried a very heavy sack that caused her to walk partially slumped over. She could barely keep it off the ground.

"Sara, what are you doing out so late?" I called as I caught up with her. The wind picked up a bit as I spoke. Suddenly, the air was cold as ice and my arms broke out in goose bumps. "May I carry your sack for you?" I added, remembering my manners. My mother would kill me if she found out I let Sara carry such a heavy load without assistance.

Silently, old Sara handed me the sack. It was so heavy I almost dropped it. I shivered again.

"What a nice boy," Sara said as we started walking up the hill. At least, I thought she said it. But the voice had come from the sack, not from the figure walking beside me.

"Wh . . . what did you say?" I stuttered.

"Such a nice boy to help an old woman," said the sack in my hands.

I dropped the sack with a yelp of terror. It rolled down the sidewalk and bumped into the iron railing in front of a house.

The head of old Sara fell out of the bag. I looked in horror from the head to the figure beside me. It threw back the shawl, revealing a bloody stump underneath it. The figure began to change, transforming swiftly from an old beggar woman to a soldier to a small child to a large black dog, all without heads.

I gave a shriek that could have shattered glass and ran uphill toward my house as if all the demons in hell were chasing me. I could hear the head laughing. It began bouncing up the hill behind me.

"Come back, good boy! Come back!" the head yelled with each bounce. The voice was getting closer, but my house was right ahead. I leapt up the steps and hit the door handle hard, hoping my mother had left it unlocked. She had. I fell in the door, right at the feet of my mother, who had been anxiously looking out the window to see if I was on my way home. She slammed the front door, and we both heard the head bounce against it and tumble away down the steps. It wailed loudly as it rolled down and down the street.

Slowly, I sat up and looked at my mother, who was leaning against the front door, breathing heavily.

"Well, young man," my mother said after a moment, "I hope that teaches you to come straight home when I call."

"Yes, Mother," I said, swallowing hard.

She helped me to my feet and got me a cup of hot cocoa from the kitchen to take up to my room. As I shakily mounted the stairs, I decided I had better rethink my position on bogeymen and maybe even ghosts in general. Perhaps I had been a bit hasty in dismissing all the stories as complete nonsense. Perhaps.

The Candle

LOS ANGELES

Something was amiss with his health lately, but he was not sure what. Sometimes a short climb up the stairs would make his heart thump painfully and cause the breath to catch in his throat. He did not want to worry his wife or children, so he said nothing about these little episodes. But he decided that he would mention them to the doctor, as soon as he had a chance to go. Things were very busy at the moment, and it didn't seem worth the bother of complaining over some shortness of breath. Still, something was not right.

Several weeks passed. He was growing alarmed by his weakness. A full day's work exhausted him so much that he had no strength left to do the nightly chores or play with the children. Everyone noticed it now. His wife insisted that he visit the doctor. They were too poor to keep a carriage and his eldest son needed the horse to get to his job across town, so he decided to walk to the doctor's clinic the next morning after the chores were done. What with one thing and another, he did not get started until close to noon, so his wife packed a satchel with a nice chicken and some bread to eat as he walked.

The chicken smelled so delicious it made his mouth water. He was looking forward to his meal. He decided to stop and light a small fire at the halfway point. He could rest awhile and warm up the chicken. Weariness overtook him sooner than he thought. He sank down at the foot of a tree, clutching his chest and breathing heavily until the episode passed. He was visiting the doctor just in time, he thought.

After several minutes' rest, he gathered some wood and lit a small fire. The chicken was soon heating up, and it smelled better than ever. As he poked at the fire with a stick, an old man walked by and asked him for a bite. He looked up at the old man, and his eyes narrowed. The old man seemed too big somehow, as if something supernatural were trying to disguise itself. One of the gifts handed down in his family was the ability to recognize spirits, and he knew at once that the old man was really Saint Peter, walking the earth in disguise to test the good and punish the evil. He had long despised Saint Peter, since he was not fair in his dealings with the poor. He said: "I will not give you my chicken to eat. You do not treat the poor as well as you do the rich. The rich have so much, but the poor have nothing at all." Recognizing the justice of his words, Saint Peter walked away.

A second man approached the fire as he was turning the chicken on the spit. The man asked for a taste of his chicken. He recognized the man as Saint Anthony, and said: "I will not give you a bite, Saint Anthony, because your bishops receive so many offerings, but they do not share the money with the poor." Recognizing the justice of his words, Saint Anthony walked away.

An emaciated old woman approached the fire just as he removed the chicken from the spit and asked him for a bite of his chicken. He immediately recognized her as Death. He handed her a chicken leg, saying, "Please take and eat of my chicken, Lady Death. You do not play favorites, but take the souls of both rich and poor."

Lady Death sat down companionably beside him, and they ate the chicken and the bread together.

"Where are you going?" Lady Death asked him.

"I go to visit the doctor," he told her.

Lady Death shook her head. "You do not have time to visit the doctor," she said. "Your life light grows dim." She waved a hand. The world around them grew dark. Within the darkness, he could see lights glowing in every house around them. "They are life lights," Lady Death said. "The brightest lights are the children; the weakest are the old and dying. See, there is your house. The life lights of your children are strong, but your candle flickers and will soon go out. Because you have shown kindness to me, I will give you this candle. Take it straight to your home, light it using your life light, and put the candle in its place. You must hurry, for your light is fading."

As she spoke the last words, Lady Death disappeared. He looked at the small white candle in his hand. Around him, the world regained its sunlight, motion, and color. Yet through the bustle, he could still see the life lights glowing in each house.

He put out the fire, picked up the satchel, and hurried back the way he had come. He held the candle tightly and broke into a run. Around him, the scenery with its glowing life lights blurred as he sped past. Ahead of him, he could see his house.

THE CANDLE

Five lights burned bright and steady, but the sixth light was flickering wildly. He ran up to the door, wrenched it open, and raced up the staircase. He stumbled as he reached the top. The candle fell out of his hand and tumbled down the steps. He gave a cry of anguish, half-running and half-sliding down the steps to retrieve it. His wife came hurrying from the kitchen, calling to find out what was wrong. He pushed her aside, scrambling around on the floor, searching for the candle. Above him, he could see his life light flickering, fading. The candle had rolled under a small side table in the hallway. He grabbed the candle and took the stairs two at a time. As he raced into his bedroom, he saw two life lights standing at the head of the bed. His wife's light glowed strong and steady, but as he ran into the room, he saw his life light sputter one last time and then extinguish. As the light died, he saw Lady Death standing at the head of his bed.

"I'm sorry," he said, as pain overwhelmed him.

"I also," replied Lady Death.

His wife found him lying on the floor, a small white candle clasped in his hand. He was dead.

Tommy Knockers

PLACERVILLE

I chuckled to myself as I climbed down into the darkness of the mineshaft, musing on the antics of the forty-niners who had come rushing to California to find gold. None of them knew anything about hard-rock mining. They just wanted to do a little panning, a little digging, and go home rich. Hard-rock mining was a complete mystery to them. Those of us who knew it well were looked upon as miracle workers.

They called us "Cousin Jacks." We were from Cornwall, England, and had grown up working in the tin mines. When they struck gold out in California, quite a number of us packed up everything and followed the greenhorn Yankees to the Sierra Nevada. Someone with sense was needed to teach all the so-called Argonauts how to do hard-rock mining.

We Cornishmen called that first generation of gold-seekers "farmers." They were good at placer mining—any fool can learn to pan for gold and clean out a sluice box—but heaven preserve us all when they set foot into a real hard-rock mine! The farmers were always letting strangers come onto their diggings, something a Cornishman would never do. That will jinx you for sure. Many a promising vein has pinched out after a stranger came to visit the diggings.

I settled in Hangtown and it didn't take long for me to build up a good reputation. The ease with which I discovered gold made the Argonauts think that I could smell it a mile away. Thirty years of experience in the tin mines might have helped, but I wasn't about to spoil the legend growing up around me and the other Cornish miners who condescendingly began to teach the farmers about mining.

The first thing I taught the men was to watch the candles. If the candles go out, you go out, too. A candle won't burn in bad air. If your candle flickers out, you are probably on the point of asphyxiation. I also taught them to watch the rats. Rats can sense a cave-in before it happens. "When the rats move out, so does the miner" is an inflexible rule in mining. If you watch the rats, you know which way to run. Also, no whistling in the mines. Sharp sounds cause vibrations, and vibrations cause cave-ins.

One of the farmers, a young fellow named Robert, had followed me down the shaft that morning. He took up work in a nearby tunnel. As I was sitting in the entrance to the tunnel in which I was working eating my noon meal by lantern light, Robert came along with his lunch. He sat beside me and asked me why it was that we Cousin Jacks were so good at finding gold.

"Most of us follow the sound of the Tommy Knockers," I told him.

"What's a Tommy Knocker?" Robert asked. I pointed to a small clay statue that I had placed at the entrance to the tunnel. Robert picked it up and brought it back to the lantern to

TOMMY KNOCKERS

inspect it. It depicted a little old man with a small body, a big ugly head, large ears, and a crooked nose. He wore a peaked hat, a leather jacket, and water-soaked leather boots.

"Tommy Knockers are the spirits of departed miners," I explained. "They help miners find ore. They also knock on the walls of the mines right before a cave-in. When you hear a Tommy Knocker knocking, it's best to depart the area right quick. They have saved the life of many a miner I know. Some folks say that the very first man to hear the sound is jinxed, but I haven't found that to be true, and I have heard them more than once."

"So why do you make statues of them?" asked Robert, setting the tiny man down and opening his lunch.

"Oh, it's important to stay on their good side. I always leave a bit of my lunch for them, and it pleases them when we fashion the little clay figures of their spirits. The Tommy Knockers can be spiteful creatures if they don't like you. My friend Eddie was once a target of the Tommy Knockers. They drove him crazy, pelting him with stones, stealing his tools, blowing out his lantern."

Robert smirked at me and shook his head. "It all sounds like nonsense to me. You've been working underground too long!"

I laughed. "Maybe so," I said easily. "Then again, maybe not!" To illustrate my point, I told him the following story.

Eddie couldn't figure out why the Tommy Knockers had singled him out until one day he heard a voice calling to him from the dark opening of a nearby shaft.

"Eddie, I want my five dollars!" the Tommy Knocker said.

Eddie was so startled he dropped his tools all over the

ground. The voice sounded just like that of his old friend Joe Trelawney who had died in a cave-in a few months back. Eddie had borrowed five dollars from Joe and had never returned it. Eddie went into the shaft, and sure enough there was Joe Trelawney's ghost, shrunk to the size of a two-foot dwarf with a big ugly head, large ears, and a crooked nose. He wore a peaked hat, a leather jacket, and water-soaked leather boots. Eddie could see right through him!

The Tommy Knocker was not pleased to see Eddie.

"Give me back my five dollars, Eddie!" the ghost of his old friend demanded.

"I don't have any money on me, Joe," Eddie said, patting his pockets for emphasis.

"I've heard that before," said the Tommy Knocker dryly. "I didn't believe it then, and I don't believe it now!"

The Tommy Knocker disappeared into thin air, leaving an uneasy Eddie to wonder what the ghost would do next. He soon found out!

All day long, Eddie was plagued by the Tommy Knocker. His ladder was shaken so hard that he almost fell. The loud tapping noise of an invisible drill nearly drove him mad. He just missed being buried by a rock fall. And through it all, Joe's voice would taunt him: "Give me back my five dollars, Eddie!"

"All right, Joe, all right!" Eddie finally yelled into the mouth of the tunnel where his friend had appeared. "I'll get your bloody five dollars!"

Abandoning his work for the day, Eddie made the long climb to the surface and took five silver dollars from the moneybox he kept under a loose board in his bedroom. Then he climbed back down into the mine and stuck the five dollars into a crack in the wall next to the place Joe's spirit had appeared to him.

"There's your five dollars, Joe!" Eddie shouted, his voice echoing oddly in the dark tunnel.

"It's about bloody time," Joe said, appearing next to him and peering critically into the crack where the money lay.

"Are you going to leave me alone now?" Eddie asked.

The Tommy Knocker grinned impishly at Eddie. "Maybe," he said. He scooped up the five silver dollars and disappeared into the dark.

I finished my story and sat back to take a bite of my meat pasty. Robert blinked a few times and then shook his head. "I still think you've been working underground too long," he said.

"Tommy Knockers have helped me find ore more than once," I said, gesturing toward the small statue at the entrance to the tunnel.

"That's ridiculous," Robert exclaimed. He rose and dusted off his trousers. "Keep your secrets then, old man. You Cousin Jacks have some special secret to finding gold, and I aim to figure it out."

Robert walked away, kicking the small statue as he passed. It broke in two pieces, the head landing on the far side of the tunnel. I picked up the pieces once he was gone and put them back together using some sticky mud.

"What fools these Yankees be, eh Joe?" I said to it as I carefully set it in a crevice at the entrance to the tunnel. I placed a large piece of my pasty beside the statue, saluted it with my pick, and went back to work.

A few minutes later, I heard Robert cursing loudly from inside his shaft. He'd been hit in the head with a rock. I chuckled to myself. Robert should not have kicked the statue. He had annoyed the Tommy Knockers, and they were not a forgiving lot.

Several times after that, Robert's lantern was snuffed out by a stray breeze. Over Robert's cursing, I thought I heard a soft laugh. Toward the end of the day, a shower of stones buried Robert's tools. He spent the rest of the day digging them out.

I kept working, long after Robert and the others had left for the day. I'd found a promising-looking seam that I wanted to try out.

"It turns left about five yards in," a familiar voice said to me conversationally. I glanced around. A small fellow wearing a peaked hat, a leather jacket, and water-soaked leather boots stood at the entrance to my tunnel. He was delicately eating the bit of pasty I had left next to the statue.

"Evening, Joe," I said. "How big is this seam?"

"Smallish," the little man replied. He hopped up onto a stone ledge next to the lantern and sat swinging his legs. "It peters out after a hundred yards. If you want to work the big gold-bearing quartz vein, you should start another tunnel down a few yards to the right—next to that outcropping—and go straight for ten feet. That's where you'll hit one of the source veins of the Mother Lode."

"Mother Lode?" I asked. I kept my voice calm, but my hands were shaking. I nonchalantly laid down my pickaxe and wiped my head with a rough handkerchief I kept in my pocket.

"Yes indeed. That vein is one of the biggest in these hills.

Where do you think all that placer gold came from?" the Tommy Knocker said brightly. "Well, I'm off. Thanks for the pasty, Eddie."

"Thanks for the advice, Joe," I replied.

The little man paused at the entrance to the tunnel.

"Shaft number three is going to cave in tomorrow," he said. "You might want to warn the others. *Before* we do."

"I will," I said.

The Tommy Knocker nodded and disappeared into the darkness.

I sat down shakily. Joe never steered me wrong about ore, but he'd never pointed me to a Mother Lode before. Maybe he liked hearing me tell his story to a Yankee. I went over to the place my old friend had pointed out to me and started digging.

That night, I told several of the Cousin Jacks about a potential cave-in in Shaft 3. They nodded solemnly when I alluded to the Tommy Knockers. They had been hearing some faint rapping all day long. The next morning, we warned everyone working in the mine to stay away from the shaft, since it could go any time. A few men laughed off the warning, Robert among them, and entered the shaft. We dug out their bodies as best we could after the shaft collapsed. I found Robert buried from the waist down in rubble. He would never walk again.

Later that day, I took a special meal down to the new tunnel and left it for old Joe Trelawney the Tommy Knocker. I had hit the Mother Lode of gold-bearing quartz right where the little old man had said it would be. The statue I made of him still sits in a niche I carved out for it. It always pays to stay on the good side of the Tommy Knockers.

26

To Your Health

SACRAMENTO

"Your granddaddy was fifty years old when he set out by wagon train for California. The year was 1850, and all the nation could talk about was gold," I told my little niece Emma, who was perched upon my knee. We sat on the porch in front of my house. "He was in poor health, and could not pan for gold. His plan was to set up a mercantile full of the merchandise the miners needed—food, clothes, tools for digging. He packed up his wife and two sons and they came to California. The wagon train was plagued with troubles—they were attacked by Indians, they were threatened by a tornado, they lost some of the group in a flash flood—but eventually they reached Sacramento and your granddaddy and his family opened a store."

"StanLEY!" A quavering, high-pitched voice interrupted my story. The voice had the piercing quality of an operatic tenor, and the second syllable of my name was uttered a good octave above the first, in the manner of a Swiss yodeler. I sighed and put my niece down.

"Coming, Granddaddy," I said. Little Emma did not complain, despite the interrupted story. She was only three, but

TO YOUR HEALTH

already she knew how futile it was to interrupt Granddaddy in full cry.

"StanLEY! I can't find my dad-burn glasses anywhere!" Granddaddy bustled onto the porch, waving the newspaper at me. He looked remarkably well for a man who had passed his two hundredth birthday. Yes—that's right. Granddaddy was more than two hundred years old. He was the same Granddaddy from the wagon train story I was telling Emma. Impossible, you say? I only wish it were! But like the best antiques and the family scandals, the eldest son of each generation of my family for the last one hundred and twenty years had inherited both the family estate and good old Granddaddy.

Granddaddy said it was the balmy climate of California that resulted in his good health and his long—his very, *very* long— life. Before he came to California, Granddaddy was a sick man. His health had been poor all his life, and he hadn't expected to live long enough to make his fortune when he came West. But the salubrious climate of our fair state had quickly cured him of his illnesses. Of all illnesses. It even cured his trick knee.

Grandma and both her sons had died of old age some- where in their nineties—we are a long living family—but Granddaddy just kept on going. He outlived his sons. He out- lived his grandsons. He outlived his great-grandsons. He out- lived absolutely everybody and gave no sign of ever planning to die. Now, some families would consider it a blessing to have their old granddaddy in their lives for so long. After all, he could share his wisdom and his experiences with the genera- tions and help his family lead better lives. That's what you might think.

But Granddaddy was exactly the opposite. He was stubborn. He was opinionated. He was outspoken. He had a peppery temper. He stuck his nose into everybody's business. It was either do it his way, or move very far away. And inevitably, any advice he gave you was wrong. In fact, we'd taken to asking Granddaddy for advice and then doing exactly the opposite, he was so predictably wrong in everything he said.

Granddaddy was impossible to live with and impossible to get rid of. Despite his excellent health, Granddaddy refused to have his own house. He insisted upon living with the family, since he could "go any time." He wouldn't do a lick of work around the house, and the family was made to feel guilty if they did not cater to his every whim.

"StanLEY," Granddaddy yodeled again. I went to help him find his glasses. They were, as usual, on top of his head.

Granddaddy settled into a porch rocker and proceeded to criticize everything he read in the paper, which was okay with me because it kept him from criticizing me. Lately, Granddaddy kept harping on me to marry my girlfriend, Hannah, who lived in a small house just up the street from me. I wouldn't have minded marrying Hannah, but she absolutely refused to live with Granddaddy. She insisted that it was time one of my two younger brothers took a turn caring for the old gent. Unfortunately, they also refused to live with Granddaddy. My youngest brother had gone so far as to move to New Jersey just to avoid housing the crotchety old man.

A few months went by, and I noticed a change in Granddaddy. He sighed more often, and spent a lot of time in his favorite chair, looking at old photographs. One day, I dragged a chair over and sat down beside him. "What's wrong, Granddaddy?" I asked.

"I'm old, Stanley, that's what's wrong," Granddaddy said. "It's jest not natural, outliving all my children's children's children. I miss your Granny Ethel, and my boys, and all my old friends. I miss the horse and wagon days, and the crazy miners that used to scatter gold dust all over the floor of the mercantile. I miss feeling useful." He took out his handkerchief and blew his nose. Then he showed me the picture of Granny that hung in a locket around his neck. "I should be whooping it up with yer Granny in heaven by now, and yet here I am, still here on this wicked old earth. I asked the doctor about it at my annual physical last week. He said I was so healthy I could live another hundred years."

"Well, Granddaddy, is there something you would like to do to pass the time?" I asked. "Take up a new hobby? Travel?"

"Travel," Granddaddy mused. "Now I wonder. . . . You know, Stanley, I used to be a right sickly fellow before I came to California. I didn't think I would live to see fifty-five, never you mind two hundred. Fact of the matter is, I have had extremely good health since I moved to this here balmy climate, and I haven't set foot in another state since. Maybe if I traveled to a less-desirable climate, old age might finally catch up with me!" Granddaddy paused and looked again at the picture of Granny. "Young Adam is still living in New Jersey, isn't he?" he asked.

"Yes, Granddaddy," I said, suppressing a grin at the notion of my Granddaddy going to stay with my youngest brother. Adam couldn't stand Granddaddy. They started arguing within five minutes of meeting each other, and by the end of ten minutes they stopped speaking altogether, and one of them would storm out of the room.

"Well, that's settled then," Granddaddy said, perking up. "I'll go stay with Adam for a spell and see if old Mother Nature can finally catch up with me! If I'm lucky, I'll come home in a casket, and you can bury me beside your Granny at last, Stanley. What do you say?"

"Granddaddy, you can hardly expect me to wish you dead!" I protested.

Granddaddy chuckled. "No, you are a good boy, Stanley, and I know you love me in spite of your grumbling. But you can't deny that I am standing in the way of you marrying your girl! Oh, I know all about it. She can't abide my bossing, and I am too old to change my ways. This way is best, you'll see."

Granddaddy jumped up from the chair, still as spry as a young man of twenty, and went to phone my brother Adam in New Jersey. Poor Adam wasn't given a chance to say no. Granddaddy told him in no uncertain terms exactly when he would arrive and what type of meal Adam's wife was expected to serve the first night. Then he phoned the airline and bullied them into give him a first class seat for coach fare. Before you could say "Jack Robinson," old Granddaddy was on a plane bound for New Jersey, and I was free to do as I pleased. I confess, I missed the old man, though it was nice to have Hannah over as often as I wished without the inevitable clashes she used to have with Granddaddy. It was such a pleasant interlude that I finally dared to propose and Hannah accepted.

Then the news came from New Jersey. Granddaddy had taken a turn for the worse. Within a week, Granddaddy had passed away of extreme old age. Adam was all choked up when he called me. It seems he and Granddaddy had managed to bury the hatchet just before the end.

Granddaddy's last wish was to be buried in California. Adam and his family flew out with the body, and we planned a huge funeral, full of flowers and a vast number of Granddaddy's descendants. It was a sad time. We gathered in the church around his flower-strewn coffin, weeping and reminiscing. Hannah sat holding my hand. Even she wept for the old man who had delighted in tormenting her very existence.

Just as the preacher was winding up his eulogy, there came a thunderous knocking from the inside of the casket! Everyone jumped and several of my older cousins screamed. The knocking sound came again. Then Granddaddy's voice yodeled: "StanLEY! Stanley! Let me out of this dad-burned coffin, will you boy?"

I leapt to my feet and rushed to the casket. Together, Adam and I lifted the cover. There was Granddaddy, blinking at us and sitting up, as rosy-cheeked and healthy as the day he left California.

"But you were dead!" I exclaimed, not knowing whether to cry with relief or stamp my foot in frustration. This was so typical Granddaddy.

"Yep, I was!" Granddaddy said, grabbing Adam and me by our shoulders and leaping nimbly out of the coffin. "I was just setting down to a cup of tea with yer Granny when suddenly my spirit was whipped right out of heaven and back into my body. It's this dad-burned healthy air in California. It cured me lickety-split."

Granddaddy bowed to the assembled mourners. "Sorry to put you folks to so much trouble," he said to his descendants. "Take some of these flowers with you when you go."

He turned to me and whispered: "You have a funeral lunch planned, don't you?" I nodded, too amazed to speak. Granddaddy straightened up and announced: "I'll see everyone for lunch at one o'clock over at Stanley's place. Now be off with you!" Granddaddy was still as bossy as ever! He hurried the assembled relations out of the church. In a matter of moments, only Adam, Hannah, and I remained behind. Hannah was comforting the pastor and the funeral director, who were both overcome with shock.

"You seem to be taking this rather well," I said to Granddaddy. "I thought you wanted to be with Granny in heaven."

"I do, lad, I do," said Granddaddy. "Heaven was a grand sort of place, and yer Granny is prettier than a picture. But I reckon the Good Lord must have sent me back for a reason. So I'll just have to bear up and wait until my appointed time comes."

"Now just a minute, old man!" Hannah said, coming to join us. "I do not begrudge you your extended life, not one bit. But I insist on you living in your own house while you remain healthy. Stanley and I have waited long enough to get married, and we are not going to wait another minute."

Granddaddy chuckled delightedly. "All right then, girl. Do you have a place for me to stay?"

"You can live in my house. It's just down the block from Stanley's place; close enough to visit every day, but far enough away for us to have some independence."

"Done!" Granddaddy said. He and Hannah shook hands. Then we all went back to my place and ate a splendid funeral lunch.

The Evil Eye

MONTEREY

I had a good job in those days, working as an attaché for Comandante Hermenegildo Salvatierra. At the time these events took place it was the rainy season in the year of our Lord 1797. I was still new to my position, but I was quickly learning my post. The Comandante was a good master. He treated his soldiers and his servants like an indulgent parent.

Comandante Salvatierra was both an intelligent man and a wise one, a combination that is not often found in one person. His appearance was marred by the fact that he was missing one eye, which had been shot out by an arrow in battle. The loss had not hampered him in any way, although, knowing him to be a proud man, I suspected that he disliked appearing in public with only one eye.

One day, the Comandante told me that he was expecting someone from Salem to arrive with a package for him. When he came, I was to usher him directly to the Comandante without question. I kept watch for this man and was deeply immersed in my paperwork when Captain Peleg Scudder of Salem was brought into my office. He was a jolly, round fellow with an engaging manner. I quite liked Americans. I did not see many, for the law forbade any extended stay of American ships in Spanish waters. We exchanged greetings, and I ushered the roly-poly captain into the Comandante's study, where the Comandante greeted him like a long-lost brother. He was offering the man a drink when I quietly made my exit.

From time to time I heard laughter and song coming from the inner sanctum. Finally, the Comandante and the captain emerged, and parted ways with sadness. I wondered what it was the captain had brought for the Comandante, for I had seen no package in his hand, nor did he have room on his person to carry more than a small item. It wasn't until the next morning that I found out.

The following day was Sunday. I was sitting in the pew with my lovely wife, Maria, when the Comandante entered the church and took his place. The congregation murmured in astonishment at the sight of him, for he was now in possession of two eyes instead of one! So that was what the American captain had brought him, I mused.

The priest hurried to the Comandante, exclaiming over the miracle that had been granted to the fortunate man. I chuckled to myself, realizing that the priest and the local residents all thought the Comandante's new eye was real. No one in either the presidio or the mission had ever heard of a glass eye.

During the next few days, I heard stories circulating about the Comandante's new eye. The priests were using the miraculous appearance of his right eye as an example of the effect of good works and prayer. It made quite an impression on everyone.

At first, people went out of their way to speak to the Comandante and marvel at his new eye. Then I noticed a change. The soldiers manning the presidio were not used to looking into a false eye. The glass eye had a cold, stern appearance that did not match the warmth of the Comandante's real eye. It made people nervous. After a harrowing interview with the Comandante, I heard the town drunk tell his neighbor: "The Comandante's new eye, it seemed to see into my soul. It called forth grave confessions of sins that I have not even told to my priest. Truly, it is an evil eye!"

It did not take long for his words to circulate to every home in the presidio. It was rumored that the new eye had been given to the Comandante by the devil, and many became afraid to speak to him. Even his friends started avoiding the Comandante. Those soldiers whose business took them into his presence treated him with suspicion and would speak only those words necessary to complete their transactions. Even my Maria believed the stories. I told her that it was a fake eye, made out of glass and brought to the Comandante from America. Maria said she did not care if it was made out of diamonds, it was an evil eye and no good would come to me while I worked under its baleful stare.

Salvatierra was upset by the change he sensed in the people of the presidio, although he did not know its cause. He began withdrawing from society. Slowly, his easygoing, indulgent manner changed. In his official dealings, he became harsh and exacting. In his personal life, he acted like a spoiled, ill-tempered child. Several times, I broached the topic of his new eye, trying to tell him that it made people nervous. But he would not listen to me.

THE EVIL EYE

One of the old men who attended the local mission, a man called Nico, was especially terrified by the Comandante's evil eye. Nico had been a special favorite of the Comandante and had taken the change in his personality very much to heart. I did not realize it at the time, but Nico was determined to save the Comandante from the evil eye that the devil had bestowed upon him. He decided that he would poke out the Comandante's right eye and thus restore him to his former state of grace.

One night, while I was working late on some papers that were due to sail out on a ship the next day, Nico crept into the Comandante's garden and made his way to the bedroom window. Nico slipped over the windowsill and stood looking down at the Comandante, who was asleep in his bed. Suddenly, he gave a howl of terror. The Comandante's real eye was closed in slumber but his right eye was wide open and it glared at him in the light of the full moon.

When I heard Nico scream, I ran out of the office and down the hall to the Comandante's bedchamber. Comandante Salvatierra, awakened by the noise, had grabbed his sword and was flailing wildly at Nico. The old man managed to land a punch in the Comandante's right eye before I could stop him. I made a grab for Nico and finally managed to subdued him.

I took away the sword away from the half-asleep Comandante before he could accidentally decapitate me. I could see that his right eye was cracked by the blow from Nico's fist. Then I lit a candle and turned to glare at Nico, who was huddled in terror on the floor.

"What in the world is going on?" I shouted at Nico. He pointed a shaking hand at the Comandante's ruined right eye.

"I have destroyed the evil eye," he said to me. "The Comandante is saved."

Comandante Salvatierra fingered his ruined glass eye ruefully. "You think this is an evil eye, Nico?" he asked.

"The eye is darkened now and will do evil no more," the old man said solemnly.

"No wonder everyone has been avoiding me," Comandante Salvatierra said to me. "You were right about this eye, my boy."

I picked Nico up off the floor and frog-marched him out of the house and down the road to the mission, scolding him all the way for punching the Comandante and ruining his glass eye. I don't think he was listening to me. He had the beatific look of a hero who has accomplished his mission against great odds. I turned him over to the priest, who gave him a tongue-lashing for his behavior. But I could tell that the priest was secretly relieved to hear that the evil eye had been destroyed.

There was great rejoicing in the presidio when people saw the Comandante's cracked and darkened right eye. The evil eye was gone, and the people started trusting him again. The Comandante's kind and gentle manner returned. Once again, he acted like an indulgent parent toward all. He wore the broken glass eye for the rest of his life. And he never told anyone that the eye they had all feared was just a trinket that a sea captain had brought him from America.

Bigfoot

WILLOW CREEK

I finished the last of my beer and paid my tab. My friend Harry was sitting at the bar telling the bartender his latest fishing story, but I knew he wouldn't be staying much longer, either. We were going hiking early tomorrow morning, and he liked to get a good night's sleep before a hike.

Harry and I are the only two in our circle of friends who like to hike. While our buddies stayed up late drinking and playing pool, Harry and I got up early and hit the trails. Humboldt County has some good hiking trails, and we knew them all. They call this beautiful territory "Bigfoot country," and I was a firm believer in the Sasquatch, though I had never personally met one. But not Harry! No, he was a firm unbeliever; a fact I found puzzling because Harry had lived most of his life in these parts and most of his family had met the big fellow or one of his friends at one time or another.

"Going hiking tomorrow, Ben?" Chuck Thompson called out from his spot at the pool table.

"Yep. Harry and I are taking a hike up along Bluff Creek," I said.

"Going to see Bigfoot?" he asked.

"Not if I can help it," Harry called from his seat at the bar. "I think it's insane the way you guys all believe in that old story."

"Your wife believes in Bigfoot," I said. "To hear her tell it, he walked right into your front yard one morning."

"She claims that he tried to follow her into the house," said Harry. "But, my friend, I didn't see him at the breakfast table that morning."

"You saw his footprints in the yard," I retorted.

"I saw a blurry spot next to the driveway that looked a lot more like a hole in the ground than Bigfoot's footprint," said Harry the Unbeliever.

"Give up, Ben!" Chuck said. "You'll never make a believer out of him. Bigfoot could walk right into the bar and shake his hand, and he still wouldn't believe."

"If he bought me a couple of rounds, I'd believe in him," said Harry. We all laughed and then shook our heads at our poor, misguided friend. Harry and I arranged to meet up at his place in the morning and carpool to our hiking destination. Then I got into my car and drove home to Willow Creek.

I told my wife about the conversation at the bar when I got in. Sharon said, "Wouldn't it be great if you and Harry bumped into Bigfoot tomorrow? That would really shake his disbelief!"

"What are the chances of that happening?" I asked. "Bigfoot never shows up when you want him to."

"Too bad," Sharon said, and I agreed.

I got up at the crack of dawn and drove to Harry's place to

pick him up. Sharon had packed enough food to feed an army and as we drove the smells coming from my backpack were so delicious that I was tempted to start eating lunch right then and there, but I refrained. We arrived at the trailhead, and Harry and I walked along the rugged path leading into the woods, chatting off and on as the mood struck us. It was a sunny day, but not too hot. Perfect for hiking.

The path narrowed a bit as we neared the creek. I surged out in front, listening with enjoyment to the sound of the water flowing in the creek and the chirping of the birds overhead. Suddenly, a strange, rotten smell drifted through the air. I wrinkled my nose as I rounded the bend and then stopped dead in my tracks. Standing beside the creek was a huge apelike figure with a hairy body, long arms, and a flat brown face. Its eyes were round and dark, its ears were small, and its nose was flat.

I gasped aloud. Then Harry cannoned into me from behind, nearly knocking me over. The creature fled into the woods. It was as fast as a bolt of lightning.

"Hey, watch it!" Harry said. "Why'd you stop like that? Did you see Bigfoot?"

"As a matter of fact, I did," I said coolly.

Harry smirked at me. "Sure you did," he said.

I walked over to the place where the Bigfoot had been standing when I came around the bend and pointed at the ground. "All right, explain these," I said, pointing at a set of sixteen-inch footprints heading off toward the trees. The strides were a good four feet in length and the footprints were deep enough to belong to a creature weighing several hundred pounds.

BIGFOOT

Harry crouched beside the footprints, studying them intently. I kept my eyes on the woods where the Sasquatch had disappeared. Sometimes they lingered in an area, watching humans with as much interest as we watched them.

"A big bear," Harry suggested after a moment. I looked at him disbelievingly. "Oh, all right, not a bear," he said. "It was probably just some kid, fooling around. Come on, I'll show you."

He jumped up and followed the footprints into the woods. I stared after him in amazement. Only a true skeptic (or an utter fool) would follow a Sasquatch right into his home territory. I trailed after him slowly, ready to run if there was any sign of trouble.

"The ground is too hard here for any clear prints," Harry called back to me. "It looks like the kids went into the bushes. How much do you want to bet that the Bigfoot prints go into the bushes and boot tracks come out the other side?"

Harry parted the bushes and went through. As he did so, I caught another whiff of rotten garbage. There was a moment of silence. Then I heard Harry give a strangled yell, which was echoed by an equally startled howl of surprise. Harry shot out of the right side of the bush, and the Bigfoot leaped out of the left. They both stopped a moment and looked over their shoulders. Catching each other's eye, they both yelled again and ran away in opposite directions.

I stood stock-still, staring first one way at the fleeing Sasquatch and then the other at my fleeing friend. Harry was making good time. At his present rate of speed, I estimated that he would make it back to the car in less than an hour. I looked again at the Sasquatch. It, too, was making excellent time. I watched as it leapt over the creek in a single bound and disappeared into the trees. The smell of rotten garbage faded away.

I shrugged my shoulders philosophically and started back down the trail toward the car. I wondered how Harry the Unbeliever was going to explain away that little encounter. I walked the entire length of the trail without catching sight of Harry. I found him sitting in the car, drinking his way through one of the six-packs that Sharon had included with our lunch. After taking a look at his pale face, I decided not to say a word about the Bigfoot. I just started up the car and drove back to Harry's place while he devoured all the sandwiches and got drunk. He started muttering to himself about halfway home, but as he didn't finish any of his sentences, I couldn't answer him. I chivvied him up the steps to his house, explained the situation to his startled wife, and went home to tell Sharon about my first Bigfoot sighting.

When I got to the inn Monday evening after work, Harry was sitting at his usual spot at the bar. As I entered the room, I heard him describing his Bigfoot encounter to an enthralled group of listeners. Of course, he wasn't telling the story the way I remembered it. I didn't think the Bigfoot was ten feet tall, and I was also pretty sure it didn't have fangs. And unless I was mistaken, I was fairly certain that it wasn't me who fled to the car when I met the big guy. Other than those minor details, his story was fairly accurate.

Harry caught a glimpse of me and flushed slightly.

"Hey, Ben! I hear you ran all the way back to the car when

you saw Bigfoot!" Chuck called out when he saw me standing in the doorway.

"I felt it was my duty to call in the sighting right away," I responded lightly. Harry smiled apologetically at me.

"Was it really ten feet tall?" asked the bartender.

"Seven or eight at least," I said, "and boy did he smell!" I sat down next to Harry. "It gave me quite a shock to see him."

"Me too," Harry agreed, signaling the bartender to get me a beer. Our friends crowded around, throwing questions at me until I begged for a breather in which to drink my beer. When at last the story had been told to everyone's satisfaction, Harry rapped the bar for silence.

"Well, gentlemen," he said, lifting his glass. "I am man enough to admit that you were right and I was wrong. Here's to Bigfoot."

We raised our glasses solemnly and drank a toast to the Sasquatch.

The Devil's Pet

ELIZABETH LAKE, LOS ANGELES COUNTY

It was rumored that the devil himself had made the lake. Standing upon the mountains, he made fire and brimstone descend into the low places, filling each crack and crevice. Underneath the fiery lake, a haven was made for the devil's favorite monster, a beast of terrible proportions with the wings of a giant bat, the body of a dragon, a round, flattened head, and the crafty eyes of a serpent. The Native people living in the vicinity claimed that the lake itself was a passage to the underworld.

When the fires went out, water crept into the cracks and crevices of the valley, creating a lovely, placid lake. But evil still haunted the calm waters, and the monster continued to live in the home the devil had built for it. The monster would sleep deeply for many years and then suddenly wake, hungry and angry, and emerge into the world above. It would rise up through the mud and water of the lake and fly high above the mountains, searching for something to devour. When the monster awoke, people would flee into their homes, barring the doors and windows and keeping quiet, hoping to avoid the notice of the devil's pet.

THE DEVIL'S PET

For many long years the settlers shunned the lake. None dared to live on its shores. Finally, a Spaniard named Don Pedro Carillo dismissed the stories of a curse and built a large ranch house right upon the shores of the lake. But those who invade the devil's territory must pay a price. Three months after building his ranch, a terrible fire burned it to the ground; house, barn, and outbuildings were gone in one night. Don Pedro fled from "La Laguna del Diablo" and never returned.

For the next twenty years, the lake was carefully avoided by the people of California. Then, in the mid-1850s, a few rugged American settlers tried their luck on its haunted shores. One by one, they crept back to the civilized lands, driven away by horrible screams, unnatural noises, frightening visions that they could not explain, and terrible experiences that they would not relate to another soul. But one fact they made very clear. Something lived in the lake. Something wicked and cruel. Something it was best not to disturb.

The next to try his luck at the lake was Don Chico Vasquez. Aware of the rumors, he built his home inland and ranched all the surrounding territory. For many months, the lake remained quiet and still. Then one evening there came a terrible screeching sound. It pierced and echoed through the air, making the horses rear, the cattle bellow in fright, and the ranch dogs howl. Vasquez came running out of the house, trying to locate the source of the noise. Moments later, the range boss came galloping up to report the appearance of a demon, the likes of which had only ever been heard of in song and story.

The two men rode to the lake. As they approached the waters, an overwhelming stench filled the air, making them gasp and choke. The men saw the waters of the lake churning, and the terrible sound grew louder until it burned their ears, driving painfully into their brains like shards of ice. They clapped their hands to their ears in agony.

As Vasquez and his ranch boss watched the torrid waters, a monster broke through the surface, its huge, batlike wings flapping the air, its legs kicking up mud from the bottom of the lake. Great gusts of wind from the giant wings pressed against men and horses. The wailing of the monster grew even louder. Rearing in panic, the horses wheeled and ran back the way they had come, their riders clinging desperately to the reins as they made for the safety of the ranch house.

The sound stopped as suddenly as it had begun. In the silence, the men could hear the whoosh of great wings flapping overhead. Night was falling fast, and Vasquez did not choose to return to the lake until dawn. In the morning, a heavily armed Vasquez and his ranch hands searched the shores of the lake for a sign of the monster, but they found nothing. Later that day two head of cattle disappeared from the field. The next day it was a prized horse. Other animals soon went missing, and a giant, winged shadow passed over the house each evening just before dark. Once, the ranch boss reported seeing the monster hovering over the lake with a dead steer in its claws.

Bullets did not faze the creature; they just bounced off the monster's thick hide. Several ranch hands quit their jobs without notice, afraid to stay too close to the monster. Vasquez's losses were so great that he finally sold his ranch to a Basque immigrant named Miguel Leonis. Vasquez left the lake, never to return.

The new owner was a formidable man that no one—man nor beast—dared to cross. Leonis had no time for monsters or for the people who feared them. The day the sale was finalized, he sent men out to the lake to work his new property, though he did not go himself. For many months, there was no sign of the monster. Then the ranch crewmen began reporting that the beast had arisen from the lake and was raiding the stock pens. Leonis was furious when he heard the news. He was not about to take a loss in profit lying down. The massive Leonis grabbed his rifle and camped out on the lakeshore the same night the report reached him, waiting for the monster to appear.

It was dusk when the monster burst forth from the lake and flew into view. Leonis leapt from his hiding place with a horrible war-whoop. His scream startled the beast so much that it back-winged in confusion. Berserk with rage, the mighty Leonis ran straight for the monster's head, roaring louder than any lion and letting off random shots with his rifle. The beast landed with a loud thump on the ground, mesmerized by the ferocity of the huge man approaching it. Leonis leapt right into its face, smashing the butt of his rifle against the beast's nose and forehead, and putting a fist into its left eye. The monster started wailing and shaking its head. It tried to beat Leonis away with its long bat-wings, but the mighty rancher just kept pounding the monster with his rifle, screaming threats and curses and pushing it back towards the lake.

The monster had never encountered such hostility before. In all the years it had lived at the lake, its terrifying outward appearance had been enough to scare away all other predators.

The monster had never before been forced to fight for its right to hunt this territory. Confused and upset by Leonis' attack, the beast finally managed to shake off the terrible man and retreated to the lake. Whimpering and rubbing at its damaged eye, it disappeared underneath the muddy waters.

After that, the monster slept for many months while its damaged eye healed and the lake was still and peaceful. Then one evening, a ranch crewman riding on the shore saw the waters part and the monster burst forth from the depths. The monster flew gracefully up and up into the twilight sky, heading east until it was out of sight over the horizon, searching for a new, Leonis-free territory to hunt.

Several weeks later, an amazing story appeared in an Arizona newspaper. A monster had been seen flying over the Huachuca Mountains near Tombstone. The monster was nearly 150 feet long, with the wings of a giant bat, the body of a dragon, a round, flattened head, and the crafty eyes of a serpent. Two enterprising ranchers who lived in the area lured the beast into a trap and killed it. From that time onward, the devil's pet was never again seen at the lake.

30

They Are Going to Hang You for This!

SAN DIEGO

Don Pedro sat bolt upright in bed with a yell of anger. Dona Luisa turned over. "What is it, husband?" she asked.

"That no-good fox is after our chickens again," Don Pedro exclaimed. "Just listen to them squawking! There will be none left in the morning."

He jumped out of bed and ran to get his rifle. Stalking outside in his nightclothes, Don Pedro hurried toward the chicken coop. In the shadowy darkness, he could see a dark figure creeping away with a struggling chicken. Taking aim, he shot once, twice, three times. The figure fell to the ground and the chicken escaped, squawking in terror and running in circles.

Dona Luisa appeared with a lantern in her hand. "Did you get the fox?" she asked.

"Shot him three times," Don Pedro said proudly. "Right there."

He walked over to the dark form on the ground and

turned it over with his foot. Then he gasped in fear. It was a man, not a fox! He recognized the chicken thief as Felix Maria, a shifty ne'er-do-well who had never worked a day in his life.

"My husband, you have killed him!"

"He was stealing my chickens!" Don Pedro protested.

Dona Luisa wrung her hands. "Madre de Dios! They are going to hang you for this! We must do something!"

"What can we do?" asked Don Pedro.

Dona Luisa brightened. "My husband, I have an idea!" she exclaimed.

***

Enrique sat bolt upright in bed. His wife, Dona Estella, turned over sleepily. "What is it, husband?" she asked.

"There is someone trying to break into this house!" Enrique exclaimed.

"A bandido!" Dona Estella cried. Enrique jumped out of bed and ran to get his rifle. Creeping around the outside of the house in his nightclothes, he saw a dark figure leaning menacingly against his front door. Taking aim, he shot once, twice, three times. The figure fell to the ground.

"Enrique, are you all right?" cried Dona Estella from inside the house.

"I have shot the bandido!" Enrique shouted. "Bring me a light!"

Dona Estella appeared with a lantern in her hand. Enrique walked to the dark form on the ground and turned it over with his foot. Then he gasped in fear. This was no bandido! It was Felix Maria, the shifty ne'er-do-well who had never worked a day in his life.

THEY ARE GOING TO HANG YOU FOR THIS!

"My husband, you have killed him!" cried Dona Estella.

"He came menacing my house at night!" Enrique protested.

Dona Luisa wrung her hands. "Madre de Dios! They are going to hang you for this! We must do something!"

"What can we do?" asked Enrique.

Dona Estella brightened. "I have an idea!" she exclaimed.

***

Tom sat bolt upright in bed. Something he had eaten for dinner had not agreed with his stomach, and nature was calling. The American cowboy jumped out of bed, dressed, and hurried to the privy in back of the bunkhouse.

It was occupied by a stranger.

"Hurry up, I ain't got all day!" Tom said to the stranger, rocking back and forth from foot to foot in his predicament. The stranger did not respond.

"Some of us have got to go, partner!" Tom insisted.

The stranger did not answer. Tom drew his pistol.

"Get off the pot, Jack, or I'll shoot you!" the cowboy shouted, now in dire straights.

The stranger did not respond. Tom grabbed the stranger by the hair, knocked his head against the wall, threw him down on the ground outside the privy, and shot him in the leg for good measure. Then he jumped over the doorstep and pulled the door closed.

When he got out of the privy, the American cowboy walked to the dark form on the ground and turned it over with his foot. Then he gasped in fear. He recognized Felix Maria, the shifty ne'er-do-well who had never worked a day in his life.

"Gosh almighty, I've killed the feller," Tom exclaimed.

"They are going to hang me for this! I gotta do something!"

Then the cowboy had an idea.

***

Lorenzo had had a long night. His bar was full of drunken cowboys and shifty gamblers, which was typical. But he felt a bit uneasy about Felix Maria, the shifty ne'er-do-well who had never worked a day in his life. The man was sitting at the bar with a ghastly grin on his face. He could barely keep himself upright. Lorenzo was sure he must be drunker than a lord. The strange thing was, Lorenzo could not remember serving any drinks to the shifty ne'er-do-well that night.

Just then, a belligerent gunfighter turned to Felix and said: "I don't like the way yer looking at me, mister. You just stop staring at me and go back to yer drinking, if you know what's good fer you."

Felix grinned vacantly at the gunslinger and didn't respond.

"I'm warning you, mister. Keep staring at me and you'll regret it!"

Felix didn't respond.

The gunslinger whipped out his pistol and let fly—one, two, three times. Felix kept grinning as he slowly fell off the bar stool and hit the floor.

Lorenzo peered down at the ne'er-do-well. "You just shot an unarmed man," he told the gunslinger. "They are going to hang you for this!"

The gunslinger shifted uneasily. "I just nicked him!" he said. "The sawbones will patch him up in a jiffy. What happened, see, is he fainted on account of he was so afraid of me. I'll just take him over to the doctor's place, lickety-split."

The gunslinger picked Felix up and carted him outside. Then he had an idea.

***

It was late and Johnny was sleepy. The wagon ride had never felt so long before. He was looking forward to getting home to his bed. He whipped up his horses at the edge of town and started down the road that led to his house.

There came a sudden yell and a figure fell right in front of his wagon. Johnny shouted and reined in his horses. Grabbing his lantern, he jumped down from the wagon and hurried back to the dark figure lying on the road. He turned it over with his foot. Then he gasped in fear. He had just run over Felix Maria, the shifty ne'er-do-well who had never worked a day in his life. It looked like the man was dead.

"Mister, I saw the whole thing," the gunslinger said, riding up on his horse. "You ran him over with your wagon. They are going to hang you for this! You are supposed to watch out for drunks!"

"What am I going to do?" Johnny asked the gunslinger.

"I don't know, mister. That's your problem," the gunslinger replied, and rode off into the darkness.

Johnny picked up the corpse of Felix Maria and propped the man up next to him on the seat of the wagon. He drove away from town, wondering what to do. Then he had an idea.

***

Don Pedro sat bolt upright in bed. Dona Luisa turned over. "What is it, husband?" she asked.

"That no-good fox is disturbing our chickens again," Don Pedro exclaimed.

He jumped out of bed and ran to get his rifle. Outside in his nightclothes, Don Pedro hurried toward the chicken coop. In the darkness, he stumbled and almost fell over the figure of Felix Maria, the shifty ne'er-do-well who had never worked a day in his life.

Dona Luisa appeared with a lantern in her hand. "What is it, husband?" she asked.

"Felix Maria is back," said Don Pedro.

Dona Luisa wrung her hands. "Madre de Dios! We must do something!"

"What can we do?" asked Don Pedro.

Dona Luisa brightened. "Husband, I think you will have to pay another visit to our friend Enrique!" she said.

Resources

Botkin, B. A., ed. *A Treasury of American Folklore*. New York: Crown Publishers, 1944.

———. *A Treasury of Western Folklore*. New York: Bonanza Books, 1975.

Brunvand, Jan Harold. *The Choking Doberman and Other Urban Legends*. New York: W. W. Norton, 1984.

———. *The Vanishing Hitchhiker*. New York: W. W. Norton, 1981.

Chalfant, W. A. *Gold, Guns & Ghost Towns*. Stanford: Stanford University Press, 1947.

Clark, Ella E. *Indian Legends of the Pacific Northwest*. Los Angeles: University of California Press, 1953.

Coffin, Tristam P., and Hennig Cohen, eds. *Folklore from the Working Folk of America*. New York: Doubleday & Co., 1973.

Erdoes, Richard, and Alfonso Ortiz. *American Indian Myths and Legends*. New York: Pantheon Books, 1984.

Erdoes, Richard. *Legends and Tales of the American West*. New York: Pantheon Books, 1991.

Forbes, A. S. S. *Mission Tales in the Days of the Dons*. Los Angeles: Gem Publishing Company, 1909.

Glassock, C. B. *Gold in Them Hills*. Indianapolis: The Bobbs-Merrill Company, 1932.

Hallenbeck, Cleve, and J. H. William. *Legends of the Spanish Southwest*. Glendale, CA: Arthur H. Clark Company, 1938.

Jacobson, Laurie, and Marc Wanamaker. *Hollywood Haunted*. Santa Monica, CA: Angel City Press, 1994.

Johnson, Susan Lee. *Roaring Camp*. New York: W. W. Norton, 2000.

Judson, Katharine Berry. *Myths and Legends of the Pacific Northwest*. Lincoln, NE: University of Nebraska Press, 1997.

Lamb, John J. *San Diego Specters*. San Diego: Sunbelt Publications, Inc., 1999.

Lee, Hector. *20 Tales of California*. Windsor, CA: Rayve Productions, 1998.

———. *Heroes, Villains and Ghosts*. Santa Barbara, CA: Capra Press, 1984.

Leeming, David, and Jake Page. *Myths, Legends, & Folktales of America*. New York: Oxford University Press, 1999.

Lyndsay, Diana. *Anza-Borrego A to A: People, Places, and Things*. San Diego: Sunbelt Publications, Inc., 2001.

Marinacci, Mark. *Mysterious California*. Los Angeles: Panpipes Press, 1988.

May, Antoinette. *Haunted Houses of California*. San Carlos, CA: Wide World Publishing, 1990.

Miller, Elaine K. *Mexican Folk Narrative from the Los Angeles Area*. Austin, TX: University of Texas Press, 1973.

Peck, Catherine, ed. *A Treasury of North American Folk Tales*. New York: W. W. Norton, 1998.

Pepper, Choral. *Desert Lore of Southern California*. San Diego: Sunbelt Publications, Inc., 1999.

Polley, J., ed. *American Folklore and Legend*. New York: Reader's Digest Association, Inc., 1978.

Reinstedt, Randall A. *Ghosts, Bandits & Legends of Old Monterey*. Carmel, CA: Ghost Town Publications, 1974.

Richards, Rand, ed. *Haunted San Francisco*. San Francisco: Heritage House Publishers, 2004.

Schwartz, Alvin. *Scary Stories to Tell in the Dark*. New York: Harper Collins, 1981.

Senate, Richard L. *Ghosts of the Haunted Coast*. Channel Islands, CA: Pathfinder Publishing, 1986.

Skinner, Charles M. *Myths and Legends of Our Own Land*, Vol. II. Philadelphia: J. B. Lippincott Company, 1896.

———. *American Myths and Legends*, Vol. II. Philadelphia: J. B. Lippincott Company, 1903.

Smith, Barbara. *Ghost Stories of California*. Renton, WA: Lone Pine Publishing, 2000.

Spence, Lewis. *North American Indians: Myths and Legends Series*. London: Bracken Books, 1985.

Wilson, Rufus Rockwell. *Out of the West*. New York: The Press of the Pioneers, 1936.

Young, Paul. *L.A. Exposed*. New York: Thomas Dunn Books, 2002.

Young, Richard, and Judy Dockery. *Ghost Stories from the American Southwest*. Little Rock: August House Publishers, 1991.

Zeitlin, S. J., A. J. Kotkin, and H. C. Baker. *A Celebration of American Family Folklore*. New York: Pantheon Books, 1982.

About the Author

S. E. Schlosser has been telling stories since she was a child, when games of "let's pretend" quickly built themselves into full-length stories acted out with friends. A graduate of the Institute of Children's Literature and Rutgers University, she created and maintains the Web site AmericanFolklore.net, where she shares a wealth of stories from all fifty states, some dating back to the origins of America. Sandy spends much of her time answering questions from visitors to the site. Many of her favorite e-mails come from other folklorists who delight in practicing the old tradition of who can tell the tallest tale.

"A thoroughly researched and beautifully written guide to our past. A huge undertaking in every sense of the word." —Brian Williams, NBC News Anchor

WHERE THE BODIES ARE

Final Visits to the Rich, Famous & Interesting

PATRICIA BROOKS

Y ou don't have to be a ghoul to enjoy graveyards. Visiting the final resting places of famous personalities and historical figures is as much a celebration of lives fascinatingly led as it is an illuminating look into the past. From the famous to the infamous, they're all here. You can pay your respects to such diverse personalities as baseball greats Joe DiMaggio and Babe Ruth, music stars Leonard Bernstein and Ella Fitzgerald, and artists Andy Warhol and Jackson Pollock. Join author Patricia Brooks as she unearths nearly a thousand intriguing characters whose legacies live on beyond the grave. You'll find detailed obituaries and sepulchral photographs, as well as information on: cemetery locations and visiting hours; availability of maps, tours, walks, and special events; original homesteads or museums located nearby. Come discover cemeteries famous for their beautiful grounds and grand monuments. You can take time to admire the ornate gates and Victorian-era statuary or contemplate the simple headstones and markers that belie the bigger-than-life personalities buried below. Just don't forget to read the epitaphs, such as "Here lies Ann Mann; she lived an old maid but died an old Mann," or the classic "I told you I was sick." This wonderful book, full of history and amusing anecdotes, is a spirited guide to cemeteries across the United States, with hundreds of evocative profiles giving tribute to those lying below.

The Globe Pequot Press

For a complete listing of all our titles, please visit our Web site at www.GlobePequot.com.
Available wherever books are sold.
Orders can also be placed on the Web at www.GlobePequot.com, by phone from 8:00 A.M. to 5:00 P.M. at 1-800-243-0495, or by fax at 1-800-820-2329.